VOICES OF RAPE

REVISED EDITION

By

JANET BODE

FRANKLIN WATTS
A Division of Grolier Publishing
New York / London / Sydney / Hong Kong
Danbury, Connecticut

To Stan Mack

Voices of rape / by Janet Bode. — Rev. ed.
Includes bibliographical references and index.
Summary : Uses first-person accounts of both rape survivors and offenders to depict the physical, psychological, and legal aspects of rape and gives advice on what can be done in various situations.
ISBN 0-531-11518-6 (lib. bdg.)   0-531-15932-9 (pbk.)
1. Rape—United States—Juvenile literature. [1. Rape.] I. Title.
HV6561.B63
364.15'32'0973—dc21
97-41225   CIP
                                                              AC

CONTENTS

Report

Prevention

Facts and Opinions

CHAPTER 1

RAGE AND HEALING

Half a lifetime ago, I was forced at knifepoint to a garbage dump and gang-raped. That night a part of me died. The pain pierced so deep, writing about it was out of the question.

Later, when I was no longer numb with fear and sorrow, my rage built. I found I could not *not* let the words flow. I wrote for myself; and finally I wrote for other survivors. Healing, I discovered, often grows to include the hope of helping those in a similar situation.

In a small way, I believe I've succeeded in that effort. The original edition of the book you're now reading has generated more letters than any of the dozen-plus other titles I have had published. Mailed from places such as Moriarty, New Mexico; Bangor, Maine; and Jacksonville, Florida, they contain accounts of survivors' own grief and fury, along with their questions.

Letters come, too, from incest survivors and teenagers who've been sexually molested. While this book focuses more on date rape and sexual danger from strangers, these readers see it as a good place to start gathering information.

Closest Relatives and Distant Strangers

When an editor asked me to revise and update *Voices of Rape*, I felt that I had to do it. Minute after minute, year after year, rape still occurs, perpetrated with a chilling casualness by a range of individuals that includes family members, friends, and foes. Yet for all its horror, rape remains surrounded by controversy.

Before sitting down to write this book the first time, as well as setting about the task once more, I talked to teenagers and adults about their attitudes and their feelings about sexual assault. I listened to their experiences, tape-recorded and transcribed them. Next I collected opinions and advice from various teachers, parents, and school counselors.

Face to face, over the phone, and now by e-mail, I interviewed other people directly involved with the issue: a coordinator of a Rape Crisis Intervention/Victims of Violence Program; a social worker with the Gay and Lesbian Anti-Violence Project; an educator at a detention facility for juvenile sex offenders. I felt I had to meet the people who were working to help those who had been raped *and* those who had raped. For every survivor there is also a rapist.

I also spent an afternoon with a police detective at a Sex Crimes Unit, shared lunch with the nurse in charge of the emergency room of a city hospital, and sat in offices filled with leather chairs where, one at a time, I questioned a judge, a defense attorney, and a prosecutor. Then I visited a prison to hear what a convicted rapist and his primary therapist had to say.

Finally, to create this edition, I went back and sought out all of those people—and more—over again. Where are they now, I wanted to know, and what changes have they seen in the intervening years?

Human Beings, Not Statistics
After reading and organizing my notes from these past and present meetings, I decided that in looking at the issue I want to emphasize that rape is about human beings, not statistics.

In fact, no one really knows whether nationwide a few hundred thousand or a few million people are raped yearly. All we do know is that of those raped and molested and abused, the vast majority is female.

Now as you turn the following pages, imagine you're by my side as I talk with each person. The language you read is the language I heard—not always perfect, but, I believe, always clear.

And while I planned the book to travel from the crime outward through all the experiences and attitudes survivors often face, you can read it differently. You don't have to move from beginning to end. Instead, pick whatever chapter or chapters you think speak to you most strongly and start there. The order isn't important. What matters is that the words you read help.

When you put down *Voices of Rape*, rather than feeling worse, I predict you will feel better. This is a book about survival, healing, understanding, and decreasing the numbers of this devastating crime.

CHAPTER 2

DO IT OR I'LL FIND SOMEONE WHO WILL

If you're tricked or forced into sexual activity, that's rape.

YES OR NO

"Answer yes or no to these questions," I tell the students in a ninth-grade English class. I want an idea what they think rape is, what it isn't, and why they believe it exists.

Before that day I'd had similar conversations with other middle- and high-school students, peer counselors, and members of Acting Out, a teen theater company that puts on improvisational performances about sexual assault. Regardless of what part of the country I was in, I was beginning to learn how often these teenagers' answers mirrored one another.

"Each yes or no question begins: Is it okay for a boy to force a girl to have sex if . . .?" I say. Force, we agree, can mean just words—lines like, do it or I'll find someone who will. Force can also be words backed up by a push, slap, or shove.

"Ready to start?" I ask the students, reminding them that we'll discuss their answers after we've gone through all the questions:

Is it okay for a boy to force a girl to have sex if:

- He spends a lot of money on her?
- He's so turned on he can't stop?
- She goes to his house knowing no one else will be there?
- She's had sex with other boys?
- She's drunk or drugged?
- She lets him touch her breasts?
- She says she's going to have intercourse with him, then changes her mind?
- She's wearing sexy clothes?
- They're married?

Hands shoot up around the room. Everyone's ready to talk. A boy in a T-shirt covered with the words "Life's Too Short to Dance with Ugly Women" says he answered yes to the first question.

"That's supposed to be a surprise?" says a blonde, self-described Mall Rat. "You're wearing your attitude. Knowing you, you probably picked that T-shirt since we'd be talking about rape in class today."

"I look *fine* in this shirt. About that question of spending money on a date? If I pay for things, I expect things. Like sex. I deserve it."

A girl named Sarah says, "Well, what if I buy something for the boy? Then can I force him to do whatever I want? That's the same, but you guys don't get it."

"What girls have to do is tell the boy ahead of time, 'Listen. Don't expect things just 'cause you paid for a movie,'" says Mall Rat. "We've gotta be clear before we get to the basement or the bedroom or the back seat of the car."

Sarah interrupts saying, "But that means all the responsibility is on us: Tell your boyfriend no. If you don't say no, then tell your boyfriend to use a condom. And after he says, 'No way,' what are we supposed to answer?"

"No to sex, if that's how you feel," says Carlos, a six-footer lounging in his desk back by the windows. "You girls don't want to plan for sex. If you do, you're easy. If it just happens, then it was out of your control. And that's what's confusing to a guy. Do you want us to push you? A little? A lot? If we push, is it always rape? Guys are sexual. We have a relationship, we want sex."

"Don't you understand that it's hard to say no to a guy you really like?" says Sarah.

"It's not guys' fault that if we do it, we're cool. We're players. You girls give it up—lose your virginity—and your reputations *can* go down," says a boy the others call RetroNerd.

Double Standard

"That double standard fries me, along with the next question," says a girl who looks like a dancer. "If he's so turned on he's saying he can't stop, I'd slap him where it hurts!"

The T-shirt is angry now: "If she wouldn't do what I want, I'd slap her where it hurts. In her face." And to that, several other students have something to say.

"The guy's turned on?" says Mall Rat. "So what! The worst that can happen is he gets turned off. Sometimes I think men rape women out of spite. They want to bring us down lower."

"Yo, lighten up. Don't give us this bad rap. Guys have feelings, too. We're not just a two-legged penis," says Carlos.

"Okay, not all guys are nasty," says the dancer. "But these days some of you have such emotional problems you don't know how to control yourselves. There's so much violence coming out of you, I think in some ways every girl has been raped, at least mentally. I hate all that screaming, disgusting stuff that macho guys yell at us just for walking down the hall."

"Yeah, yeah," says RetroNerd. "I wish a bunch of girls would yell at me."

"Girls play like they don't know what's what, then blame everything on us. Like look at that next question. A girl ought to realize what's in the guy's mind when it's the two of them alone at his house," says a jock wearing a white shirt, Gap jeans, and Nikes.

A girl with orange hair swivels around, glares at the jock and says, "You're saying a girl shouldn't go to a guy's house with him alone unless she walks through the door knowing she's walking into sex? That's crazy. You can have a relationship with someone, go visit him, and even though you're not going to do anything, you don't want the whole family sitting in your face."

Headlines from one spring as reported in *The New York Times*

EXPULSION URGED IN WEST POINT
CADET'S FALSE RAPE CHARGE
—April 30

4 Charged with Rape of 15-Year-Old
Bayonne (NJ) Authorities Say Teen-Agers
Committed Revenge Attack
—May 18

> ## Four Teenagers Charged in Rape of Girl in a Classroom in Queens (NY)
> —May 27

> ## Parolee Is Charged in Rape and Slaying of Long Island (NY) Teacher
> —June 4

> ## In Retrial, Darien (CT) High School Wrestling Star Is Convicted of Rape Committed 11 Years Ago
> —June 13

Gossip

"I'm not talking about 'in a relationship,'" says the jock. "I mean you've just known a girl a couple days and ask her to come to your house. She *must* know the circumstances. She's probably gossip. Everybody's whispering, 'She's had it from this boy and that boy.' It's okay then. She doesn't care."

"But if she doesn't care, it isn't rape," says the orange hair, which the jock answers with, "If she's done it with every other guy, what does it matter?"

"It matters if she doesn't want to have sex. That's rape! Anyway, you guys like someone who's a challenge. You want to prove you can take the challenge."

"You know," says the Mall Rat, "in going over these questions, I keep wondering why parents hardly ever mention rape to us, and when they do, their main advice is don't talk to strangers. It's more the ones we know, we've got to watch."

The T-shirt interrupts this time, saying he's ready with an opinion on the question about being drunk or drugged: "If she passes out, the guy can do whatever he wants. Since she won't remember, it's no big deal."

"No way!" says a girl with a gold necklace with the name Alicia on it. "That happened to my cousin. Her boyfriend told her all these lies to get her to do it. He annoyed her and annoyed her, telling her he'd leave if she wouldn't do it. Well, she didn't want him to leave, but then if there's sex, she expects him to stay. He got her drunk. They did it. Then that lowlife split to find someone new."

"At least your cousin trusted you to hear what happened. If you want to know the truth, I'd be afraid that if I told friends I'd been raped, and later we had an argument, they'd back-stab me," says the dancer.

"If my cousin was raped, I'd tell her to point out the guy," says Carlos.

"The first thing I'd do is help her get help," says Mall Rat. "You don't know for sure what her boyfriend did since she was drunk."

"Gimme a break," says RetroNerd. "Maybe Alicia's cousin really wanted it bad. Like first she invited him over. Then she let him touch her wherever. That says it's okay to go on. Maybe she did that girl thing, said yes and then no. And maybe she dressed in those clothes where you better not bend over. Tell me she's wearing them for another reason. What's a guy supposed to do?"

"Nothing!" Alicia answers. "Letting a guy touch you one place doesn't give him permission to go roaming. She changes her mind? So what. It's *her* body. What she wants is what she wants and it's up to her whether she wants to give up her body."

"Back up to the clothes," says the orange hair. "What if a girl *is* dressed sexy? Why does some guy think it's for him? Maybe she has somebody else in mind. Maybe she has no one in mind. Maybe it's the fashion. Or maybe she is interested in sex. She's still the one to pick who and when and where and how."

"I'll only have sex with a person who can show me his love," says Sarah.

"Grow up, Sarah," the T-shirt says. "You're not going to stop some guy from forcing sex. He's having fun. He's not worrying about the other person."

"Birth control and people control don't always work, and then girls say it's rape. She needs an excuse, end of story," says Retro-Nerd.

"What about this question about being married?" asks the jock. "I wrote yes. Isn't that the whole point of getting married, so you can have sex anytime you want it? That's a man's right. Right?"

WHEN IS IT RAPE?

What people think of as "real rape"—the assault by a monstrous stranger lurking in the shadows— accounts for only 1 out of 5 attacks.

. . . The experts guess— that's all they can do under the circumstances— that while 1 in 4 women will be raped in her lifetime, less than 10% will report the assault, and less than 5% of the rapists will go to jail.

Time
June 3, 1991
—by Nancy Gibbs

"No!" says the orange hair. "I put no for every question. You shouldn't have to force yourself on anyone. Forced sex is rape, right?"

The Voices of Rape

Yes, I tell her and the other students, she's right. Every one of those questions should be answered no. But lots of teenagers and adults are confused on some of the basic issues. In fact, only a third of all those I asked say forced sex isn't acceptable in any of those situations.

Lots of people are even confused about whether they've been raped. And you can be sure that many who rape—especially those who know their victims—never think of themselves as rapists.

When I go to schools to talk about sexual assault, we focus mainly on what's known as date- or acquaintance-rape situations. Most people, teenagers included, are far more likely to be raped by people they know than by strangers.

What's true, too, is the attacker may be a family member. While we usually call it incest, molestation, or sexual abuse—not rape—the act itself remains the same: one person tricking or forcing another into sexual activity.

Once the bell rings and these discussions end, a student or two always stop to talk to me. Some ask questions. Others bring up their own stories. At the end inside I feel furious. How can one human being do those things to another?

In a jumble of words a fifteen-year-old explains that when she was twelve her sister's boyfriend tried to rape her. "He had his pants down, pulled down mine, and punched me," she blurts out, before adding her mother doesn't know. She didn't tell her sister, either.

"What if a mother washes her boy and the boy says, 'Ma, no, I don't want you to. I want to wash myself.' What if she wants him to wash her, too? Is that sexual abuse?" asks a thirteen-year-old male in a voice so soft I have to lean forward to hear him. He's talking, I know, about himself.

"Yes," I answer. "That's sexual abuse."

Another student, now a junior, says that when she was thirteen, she was raped by a family friend. "My mom helped me get medical care, but now she's acting like since I've done this, I'm going to want to sleep with more guys. No way!"

A sophomore is still troubled by a friend's rape a few years ago. "Beth blames me for it," she says. "I told her, 'Don't go with those guys to that basement.' She went without me, and twenty minutes later she'd been raped."

These are just a few of the voices. Now it's time to listen to others and their firsthand accounts of rape.

Parents' Poll Shows Higher Incidence of Child Abuse

. . . Two studies released yesterday paint a bleak picture of American childhood: One estimated, based on parents' own reports, that more than three million children are punched, kicked, or struck with a hard object each year in the name of discipline, and the other, a poll of young people, found that 40 percent of girls age 14 to 17 said they had a friend their own age who had been hit or beaten by a boyfriend. . . .

. . .The Gallup poll also found that 1.3 million children a year were sexually abused. The poll did not ask parents whether they had sexually abused their children, but rather whether, as far as they knew, their children had been forced to have sex with an adult or older child, or had been forced to touch an adult or older child sexually. . . .

The New York Times
December 7, 1995
—by Tamar Lewin

17

Rape

VOICES OF RAPE VOICES OF R
APE VOICES OF RAPE VOICES
OF RAPE VOICES OF RAPE VO
ICES OF RAPE VOICES OF RAP
E VOICES OF RAPE VOICES OF
RAPE VOICES OF RAPE VOICE
S OF RAPE VOICES OF RAPE V
OICES OF RAPE VOICES OF RA
PE VOICES OF RAPE VOICES O
F RAPE VOICES OF RAPE VOI
CES OF RAPE VOICES OF RAP
E VOICES OF RAPE VOICES OF
RAPE VOICES OF RAPE VOICE
S OF RAPE VOICES OF RAPE V
OICES OF RAPE VOICES OF RA
PE VOICES OF RAPE VOICES O
F RAPE VOICES OF RAPE VOI
CES OF RAPE VOICES OF RAP
E VOICES OF RAPE VOICES OF
RAPE VOICES OF RAPE VOICE
S OF RAPE VOICES OF RAPE V
OICES OF RAPE VOICES OF RA
PE VOICES OF RAPE VOICES O

CHAPTER 3

LETTER FROM YOLANDA

Dear Janet Bode,

My name is Yolanda. I'm in the seventh grade. My best friend is 13 and she's dating a junior. She really likes him.

We were talking on the phone, she said she had her first French kiss with him. That was in December. Now it's January 4th. She was in his car driving real slow and he started kissing her. Then he put his hand up her blouse and was touching her breasts. She let him do it. I'm afraid she's going to have sex. The other day she was talking about birth control pills. I told her she was too young to get them. She said, "Oh, man, but I want to."

I don't know what to tell her, but I want to help her. I need a response soon before anything goes too far. She didn't tell her family about him. Her parents would get mad. My parents don't know about this. I couldn't tell them either.

But I do know if an older guy has sex with a younger girl even if she wants it . . . it's rape.

Sincerely,

Yolanda

Dear Yolanda,

Thanks for your letter. You gave your girlfriend good advice, even though she might not realize that right now. You want to help her see what's best. She doesn't want to listen. (She may even get mad at you.)

As long as she's confiding in you, here's what else you might do. Talk to the adults you trust the most—maybe your parents or a school counselor, a favorite teacher, a special aunt. Tell them what you told me and see what they have to say.

But remember, you are responsible for yourself and your choices; and she is responsible for herself and her choices. You can't force her to act the way you want. You can, though, keep talking to her, telling her your worries. You're saying this because she is your friend and you care about her.

Speak from the heart. You know what to say. Then, hope for the best and so will I.

Janet

CHAPTER 4

WAS IT OR WASN'T IT DATE RAPE?

Seventeen-year-old Nicole is in the middle between an older sister and a younger brother. Her parents, she knows, love her and stress what they call family time. In her home that means she'd better have a good excuse if she's going to miss dinner. Most nights they all sit down at the table together to compare their days, while eating everything from homemade pasta to carry-out.

What this high-school junior from a comfortable suburb doesn't share with her family is that she's survived two date rapes. Nicole lost her virginity to a domineering first boyfriend, and then her trust in males to her second boyfriend, David.

On a Sunday afternoon before she leaves for her video-store job, she finds the time to talk. The interview begins with Nicole's observation that only within the last six months has she realized that her sexual experiences were rape.

Because David is still in her life, she chooses to talk about him.

Confusion and Disgust

I had this long, confusing thing with myself: had I been date-raped or not? See, I've had sex—regretfully—twice. With two different people, Christopher and David. Both times it was something I really didn't want to do, and it happened and I was still protesting, and afterwards I was very upset. If I could go back, I'd still be a virgin. Now I'm disgusted with myself. What's worse yet is I still have feelings for David.

Reckless and Brutal

I met David a long time ago, maybe when I was in seventh grade. He's a year older. At first, I didn't have much of an impression of him. I thought he was nice, I guess. It's not like he was good-looking, but he was attractive. He wore a lot of Tommy Hilfiger.

Anyway, we became friends and I went out with his best friend, Christopher. It was heartbreaking for me when Christopher and I stopped dating. He was my first love. Afterwards I kept telling David, "Oh, call Christopher. Find out what I have to do to get him back."

I would confide in David, although I started to think he was reckless, even wild. He lived at home, but he didn't really have any rules. It was like he lived on his own.

See, we'd usually run into each other at a place we called "the field." I'd hang with him, talk about our friends, whatever they were doing, our relationship. It was just real slow between us. Comfortable. There was no physical contact.

Then one Saturday night, he said, "Come by my house tomorrow morning." So around twelve o'clock the next day I went over. His parents were out, but at the time I didn't think anything about that.

I should have.

Almost from the moment I came through the door, he pressured me for sex. Once I'd told him, "When a guy says to a girl he wants to make love with her, that is the ultimate."

David said, "I want to make love to you."

I guess he figured the way to get me to have sex was to say that. But since I didn't fall for it, he started to force me down. There was a lot of "come on, come on, come on." Followed by "don't worry, don't worry, don't worry."

I remember thinking, "Well, I've had sex once before. What's the difference?" Still, inside I knew I didn't want to. Then David started getting brutal with me.

Drug Linked to Assaults is Reformulated

The manufacturer of a powerful sedative linked to date-rape assaults said it had developed a way to make the drug more visible when placed in a drink.

The drug, Rohypnol, known as "roofies," has no odor, color or taste. When administered to an unknowing victim, it produces torpor and leaves the victim with little memory of what happened

The reformulated drug dissolves more slowly and releases a blue color so that it can be more easily detected. In addition, even in a dark beverage, particles of the tablet will float.

The New York Times
October 19, 1997
—AP

At the last minute the thing that got me to do it was this thought: "If I have sex with him, the relationship won't be tense. It won't be, like, this Big Decision. We'll do it and it will be over."

Afterwards, though, I realized there was a difference. I always thought you have sex and then there are bells. You fall in love or something. Instead, by then, I hurt—emotionally and physically.

Bragging Rights

Now it's, like, I want David out of my life totally. But I can't do that. For some reason I feel we're attached. I'm both attracted to him and hate him.

Guys around this school all seem to want sex. There are some girls they can brag about and some girls they can't. I was one you could brag about, so that's what he did. David told people, when he knew I didn't want him to. As soon as people found out, I was trash.

This one girl in particular picked up the story and ran with it. I hate her. All she ever thinks about is clothes. We went shopping together and I told her about it partly because I wanted my name to be cleared. She was understanding that day. The next she spread my name as a slut.

How could I reverse the talk? I couldn't say, "No, I didn't do it with him."

Finally, I had a talk with a girlfriend a year older. I look up to her. She knows what she's doing. When I explained what happened, she said, "That's date rape."

After that conversation, it became an obsession. It wasn't like it would make any difference or that I'd press any charges, but I wanted to know was it or wasn't it date rape? I took some books on rape out of the library. And there it was. I had the label. Now I knew what happened.

I went to David and said, "You know, you forced me to have sex that time. I didn't want to." When I mentioned the words "date rape," he started laughing. Then later he told me he said to a friend of his, "Oh, Nicole asked me not to f——her, but I did anyway." I felt terrible.

Promises

A lot of my girlfriends are virgins. Somebody who's had any sexual experience and somebody who hasn't can't talk on the same wavelength. They can't say, "Oh, I understand about when somebody tries to get you to do something that you don't want to do." They're basically, like, "Well, you could have avoided it."

I couldn't.

I've promised myself I am going to totally abstain from sex until I'm sure that whoever I'm with cares about me for a long time. That he's not jerking me over. I'm just going to go by that. And you know what? It comforts me to have made that decision.

Where Is Nicole Now? Nicole and David's relationship degenerated into a two-year horror show. He began routinely to push her around emotionally and physically. When he got her pregnant, at first she wanted to go through with the pregnancy and, maybe, give the baby up for adoption or have her parents raise the child.

"No way," was her mother's response, as she took her for an abortion. David had promised to go along, but instead he didn't show up. He forgot, he told Nicole. Then he disappeared from her life entirely, reappeared, repented, and hit her some more. It took another year combined with help from her increasingly concerned and upset parents, an order of protection from the police, and a teen support group that focused on violent dating relations to give her the power and self-confidence to walk away.

CHAPTER 5

WE'RE JUST TAKING ADVANTAGE OF A GIRL WHO WAS THERE

Talk to people about sexual assault and often they tell you that, yes, they agree it's rape when a stranger comes out of the night and attacks. And maybe, they add, it's rape when there's a big age difference between the offender and the victim or when there is significant physical violence.

But then they start to hesitate. They bring up what they sometimes describe as "that gray area." They have trouble calling it rape, they say, when the two people are unrelated, but know each other, and especially when they're adolescents.

It's not rape. It's just a misunderstanding, they say. It's not rape. It's just that a female wants to be pushed. It's not rape. It's just a case of the wrong people finding out.

In the following interview, Kevin explains that it's not rape. This girl is the kind who wants to have sexual intercourse with five, eight, ten teenage males one after another on the same afternoon. "The Boys," as Kevin calls himself and his friends, didn't trick her into having sex by pretending to like her.

In fact, he assures me, "Gang bangs are a common thing among teenagers everywhere." Here is his perspective of what took place those several summers ago.

—— KEVIN ——

Chicken Dinner

I turned fifteen that May. I worked during the afternoon delivering pizzas by bicycle. The rest of the time I spent hanging with The Boys. Most of us hadn't been laid yet. I know I hadn't.

What I did know, though, was that in every school there is at least one girl who gang-bangs. She loves to take on a train. In our town, the word was that Annie did. We nicknamed her "Chicken Dinner."

She was fifteen, but she told everybody she was sixteen. She lived on the other side of town with foster parents and was, I guess, pretty much disconnected from real family life.

Well, one day, Billy, my best friend, and I talked to Matt, who gave us the telephone number of a girlfriend of Chicken's. Even though we didn't know either of them, it was The Boys' idea that I call her. That summer I was the voice. I'd make all the calls. I had great charm on the phone. When I was with a girl face-to-face, I couldn't say anything. On the phone I was terrific.

The girl I called was a regular middle-class type. She'd make out and kiss, but as far as we knew, that was all. But she knew Chicken Dinner.

"Hey, I got your number from Matt," I told her. "Let's get together." I had a whole thing. It wasn't a line, but I was very good at making small talk. And then I said, "Bring Annie with you."

Billy and I knew we were going out with them because we wanted to *do it*. When we met them, my date, Pam, was a cute, chubby redhead. Chicken, though, was uck-ly. She was skinny. She had buck teeth. She had no personality—but, she f——ed.

We bought them burgers and went over to the park band shell. Nothing really happened that night. A couple nights later, Billy and I called Chicken and just the two of us picked her up. We went to the band shell again, and this time she and Billy had quick sex. He was so happy about getting laid, he started swinging like a monkey.

She liked Billy. She wasn't too crazy about me. She went knowing what would happen, and part of the agreement was me. After she and Billy finished, he said, "Okay, remember you promised to do Kevin, too." And she said, "Okay." She didn't seem too smart.

In the end I had a hard time getting it up, so I just sort of squooshed my penis around in her.

Nothing Bad Is Supposed to Happen at School

Tess speaks: The middle school I attend is mostly quiet. And up until that day, I liked being an eighth-grader. I was even given privileges. I was allowed to be a library proctor during sixth hour.

Sixth hour is never busy in the library. I was shelving books when the librarian said she had an errand to run. She'd be gone for a while. About five minutes later, I turned around and found myself inches away from another student. I tried to move out of his way, but he wouldn't let me by. "Excuse me," I said.

Instead of moving, he pushed me against the wall. I was

scared, and shocked. Nothing bad is supposed to happen at school. He took hold of my shirt and tried to take it off me. "Please, please," I remember thinking. "Let me get out of this without something worse happening." I wanted to scream, but it got caught in my throat. My fear finally outweighed my confusion.

I began to struggle. He lost his grip and I started to run. At that moment, the librarian walked in. I felt I couldn't tell her, I couldn't tell anyone. I felt "dirty." By the time I got home, my stomach was churning. I decided not to be a victim. The next day I told the librarian and went with her to let the counselor know.

The result? The guy who attacked me was expelled for two days. I felt like screaming, "Who are you kidding?! Two days!" But at least I felt I regained some power. Anyway, tell me, what more would you have done in my situation?

One Phone Call

About a month later, by the middle of the summer, The Boys started using one of the guys' rec room for our private club. His parents were never around. The room was near where I worked and sometimes I'd bike over.

One afternoon I arrived, and there were, like, eight guys taking turns with Chicken. Me, too, I decided. Afterwards, we would have these conversations with her about whose cock was bigger, whose was a better shape.

That was our basic conversation. That's all we were into. It was harmless good fun, even though I know some people have different sensitivities about this.

What happened, though, was she fell in love with one of The Boys, Matt. He was scum. He stole cars. He'd get people in trouble. She ran away from home, and when her parents sent the cops to find her, Chicken told them that Matt was the one she went to meet. The cops picked up Matt, and he immediately named everybody he could think of.

The cops came around and eventually picked up twelve of us.

You know you're allowed one phone call? Well, they didn't let us make the call. They made it for us. I was standing there while the cop was calling: "Ah, Mr. McMurtry, your son, Kevin, has just been arrested for rape."

It wasn't for "rape." It was statutory rape, quite a difference. Statutory rape means when you have sex with someone too young to be able to consent—to agree—to do it.

My father came down. At first I thought he was going to have a heart attack. He was pale as a ghost. Then he found out what was really going on. After that he was okay. He was understanding about it.

I just got myself stuck in this situation. Now I had to get "unstuck." Finally, there was a hearing, and maybe because we were all middle-class kids, they changed the charge to something like being wayward minors. We got off with one-year probation which meant we saw a probation officer once and that was it.

Taking Advantage

I ran into Chicken about two years later, and I don't think she recognized me. In my mind the whole thing was just a teenage scene. It's something that goes on. Girls have sex drives, too. And some girls like Chicken Dinner—Annie—are probably unloved and are looking for attention. What the hell? What better way of getting attention?

It wasn't sexual assault. Everybody treated her nicely. Nobody ever hit her. Everybody was friendly with her. We would buy her things. Nobody forced her to do anything. Nobody had to. We were just taking advantage of a girl who was there.

Where Is Kevin Now? Kevin didn't want to talk about this topic again. He still thinks what happened with Annie was "standard teenage stuff." His opinion remains that it happens regularly and no one gets hurt. It's more that if adults hear about it, the problems start.

Since this interview, he has attended college, graduated, married, and has the beginnings of a potentially solid career.

CHAPTER 6

WHY ARE YOU DOING THIS?

Jessica, a high-school sophomore, admits she's hard to categorize. The way she sees it, she's into flashy nails and books with titles like *The Oppression of Children*. She reads, she says, not because it's an assignment. Rather she's trying to make sense out of the world around her.

While we talk at a coffee shop, she chain-smokes Marlboro Lights. She's been trying to deal with what happened to her on that terrifying afternoon eight months earlier by not dealing with it. That approach isn't working. She considered putting her thoughts on paper, then burning the sheets to rid herself of the torment.

But Jessica could never find time. Instead, she offers to participate in this book. Maybe another rape survivor will read her story and feel less alone. Maybe a man who's convinced himself it's okay to rape might see her words and be forced to re-think his actions. She hopes so.

You look at Jessica and you see a live wire, energetic and driven. You hear her words and you marvel at her courage. Taking a deep drag on her cigarette, she exhales, leans forward, and begins her account.

—— JESSICA ——

In a Heartbeat

I had a feeling that day, like something was hanging over me. It was a Tuesday last spring. I had a test the next day. I came out of school and was on my way to work. It was two-thirty. I was wearing a pair of baggy beige pants, a black shirt with a belt, black socks, and my long black jacket.

I was standing there waiting for the bus. I could see the school from where I was. Then I noticed this older guy who looked about twenty-eight. He came out of a car and walked toward the bus stop.

He had a key chain with "BMW" on it. He had a leather jacket on, gray-and-white pants, and a black shirt. He was short and he smelled of beer.

In a heartbeat, I could feel a knife he held to my side. I tried to move, but then I felt it more. Nobody else was waiting for the bus or even on the street. Cars kept passing by.

"What are you doing?" I said.

"Don't worry," he said. "But if you move, I'll stab you." Then he started walking me to his car. I said, "No, no!" I was terrified.

He said, "I'm not playing around," and he pushed the knife more, to force me into the car. The car was blue with tinted windows, I remember that. Once inside, he blindfolded me. I kept praying and trying to think of things that would help me get through this.

First, I tried to memorize the way he was turning. Was he taking a left or a right? He started talking, telling me, "I've been watching you from my car."

Then he said, "I want you."

It felt like we had driven a mile or so from my school

35

when we came to a motel. Because he didn't want to leave me alone in the car, he told me, "We're going to the man behind the desk to get a room. Keep your head down. Don't say a word or you're dead."

Once in the office, I tried to signal the man who took the money. But it didn't work, and what was worse was that the man with the knife noticed.

Gonna Tell?

I still remember the room number, 110. He opened the door, threw me on the bed, and started tearing off my clothes. There were two beds, a TV, and a little lamp—that was all.

When he told me to get emotional with him, I said, "How can I? You're forcing me!" He slapped me, and he slapped me again. I kept thinking, "He's going to kill me."

I tried to reason with him, "Why are you doing this?"

He only said, "Just shut up and do as I say." He raped me three times.

After a while, I don't know how long, he took me in the bathroom with him. He showered, but made sure he could watch me. I was supposed to watch him, too. Every time I put my head down, he'd yell, "Look at me!"

When he got out of the shower and was going back to the room, I told him, "I'm going to use the bathroom." Instead I started to write on the mirror with my lipstick. He caught me. "I can kill you right now," he kept saying, then he added, "Gonna tell? You even think of going to the cops, I'll get you!"

Bleeding

When he was getting dressed, he dropped his business card. I couldn't believe it. Real quick, I hid it in my sock. He was probably starting to get nervous. He forgot to put the blindfold back. The next thing I knew, he stopped the car, pushed me out, and threw my book bag out behind me.

"I'll be back," he screamed and drove off.

I looked around. Dazed. I wasn't far from where I worked. I started walking, slowly. I was in pain. Crying. When I got there, I went inside and sat down. The office receptionist came over. When I told her what happened, she wanted to call the cops. "No," I said. I went to the bathroom to clean myself up. I was bleeding from inside.

I'd never had sex before.

My mother usually picked me up after work. That day when she came, she said, "What's wrong? Are you crying?" She knew I had a crush on this guy, so I told her, "I had an argument with Tommy," that's his name. She believed me.

I couldn't tell my mother what happened.

I was scared. She'd tell my father. He's really strict with me. They'd go crazy. I didn't want to see my parents suffer. I couldn't tell my sister, either. She thinks of me as her baby sister. Anyway, she'd tell my mom.

Flashbacks

I just went home. I told my mother I was tired and wanted to go to sleep. But when I got undressed, the card fell out of my sock! I'd forgotten. There was the man's name, the dry-cleaning store he owned, and its address. I got scared all over again. I thought, "Ohmigosh. I know where that is!"

I hoped I'd sleep and forget about it. But I couldn't. I kept waking up. I kept having dreams. Flashbacks, too.

The next day I went to school. I had to. I didn't want my mother to notice. And she knows I don't like to be absent. When I got there, I saw a city cop named Frank who regularly patrols around school.

I went up to him and said, "Frank, I'd like to speak to you."

He went, "What's wrong?" That's when my tears started coming down. Frank asked me questions and wrote down my answers. Then I gave him the card. He said, "I'm going to look for this guy."

"Okay, but I don't want to have to face him."

"Don't worry," he told me.

When he went to look for the man, they told him he'd disappeared. Frank told me I should make an official report to the police. He'd be there for me if I needed him. And he told

NEW YORK STATE
H.I.V. Screening Sought for Victims of Rape

Victims of rape and other crimes who may have been exposed to H.I.V., the virus that causes AIDS, should be automatically screened for the virus and offered anti-H.I.V. drugs immediately as a part of their treatment. . . . A new test can reliably detect H.I.V. in the blood three to six days after exposure, and preliminary research has indicated that the drug AZT, when administered hours after H.I.V. infection, might eliminate the virus from the body.

. . . Neither the test nor the treatment are part of current standard procedure for dealing with rape victims in hospital emergency rooms or rape crisis centers.

The New York Times
May 19, 1997
—AP

me I was brave to try to get information and remember important details.

He also said that if I wasn't going to tell my parents, I should at least talk to my guidance counselor. About a week later, I did. She sent me to a health center. A doctor checked me, and I had a vaginal infection that needed medication.

My guidance counselor told me about another place where I could go to talk it out. But I wouldn't feel comfortable telling strangers. The counselor understood, I guess, what I was trying to say. She was upset for me. She likes me a lot. She understood, too, that I couldn't concentrate on my schoolwork anymore. My marks got bad.

In fact, lots of things in my life got bad. A month after I was raped, I told Tommy, the guy I'd been dating, what happened. At first, he was mad. He said, "Why didn't you tell me right away?" But then a week or so later, we were at his house and he said we should do it.

I kept saying, "I can't. I just can't."

He was saying, "Come on, Jessica, it's me."

Then Tommy got mad. "So you let a stranger touch you and you're not going to let me?" he said.

"Don't you understand? I was forced to."

He went, "What? You want me to force it?"

"No!" I said.

We argued until he took me home and then he began avoiding me at school. Finally, I called him up, and he said, "It's over."

I asked why, and he said, "Just problems."

I realized he didn't want me, the person. He wanted sex. He said, "I thought we were going out for the fun of it." When I told him it was real for me, he said, "If I had known you were serious, I wouldn't have dated you."

The Hidden Letter

Looking at the last eight months, I've made serious changes in my life. I go to a different school now. It was too hard waiting at that bus stop. The man's words, "I'll be back," haunted me.

I wrote a letter to my family and hid it in my bedroom. It said:

"To my family,

There's something I never told you. I got raped once. I couldn't find a way to say it. Mom, please forgive me for not telling you what is too painful for me. But it would have hurt you."

Then I wrote down the man's name and the dry-cleaning store he owns. I ended, "I love you, Jessica."

I have a new boyfriend, James. He's seventeen. He dresses like a bad boy, but so far he's nice, understanding, and funny. We've been going out for two months already. Still, I'm scared of being with somebody.

He doesn't push me to have sex. In fact, James told me, "If we ever have sex, it's just going to happen." But I'm scared of having intercourse. I still get flashbacks. A lot of times when James kisses me, I feel like moving away. He goes, "What's wrong with you?" It's hard.

I have this friend. She was in school on her way to class. Some guys surrounded her. She fought back and they pushed her under the staircase.

They raped her.

They hit her.

They kicked her.

Then they ran away. She got all the way up a flight of stairs before she lost consciousness. They were classmates; guys she would have to see every day. She didn't come back to school. I saw her the other day, and she said she was still having bad emotional problems.

I'd like someone to tell me—to tell us—why do men do this?

Where Is Jessica Now? I called the phone number I had for Jessica, but the person who answered said no one by that name lived there. Her last name is a common one. When I checked with the operator, there were twenty-two entries. I started down the list and then hesitated.

I thought about our original meeting. She seemed so fragile those years ago. I felt sadness and rage that her life had been changed in this way. And then I thought about her stated goal: to help other survivors feel less alone.

Many of the letters I receive mention her story. When she speaks of her fears and her pain, other rape survivors connect with her journey. Her courage gives them courage. I decided to stop trying to find her. Instead, in my heart I hope Jessica is healthy, happy, and doing well.

CHAPTER 7

I'M TOP DOG

Michael is in jail, the Adult Diagnostic and Treatment Center (ADTC) in Avenel, New Jersey, to be exact. To meet him, I first have to be approved, then show an ID to a guard, get my wrist stamped, go through a metal detector, and be escorted past three separate clanging steel doors.

Once inside, the interview takes place in the office of William E. Prendergast, Ph.D., the psychologist in charge of the sex-offender treatment program. He sits surrounded by unsettling paintings and ceramic sculptures produced by the inmates, men who've committed incest, molested children, and raped.

The theory behind the ADTC program, says Dr. Prendergast, is what he labels whole-man therapy. "We use individual therapy, but I find that group therapy works best with sex offenders. Then because they have negative self-images, we work on their bodies. So the gym is important.

"If they haven't finished their education, we get them into school. If there's a drug problem, we deal with that, too. We also emphasize sex education, anger management, and social-skills training. Unless they develop self-confidence and self-esteem, they're not going to change. They'll start raping again—until they get caught.

"And most admit the ultimate rape is murder. Sometime during the rape, they consider killing the victim."

What about Michael? "Ask him anything. But no matter how nice these guys might appear, don't forget the other side of the story. With Michael, you'd never guess the damage he did, especially to his second rape victim. Here he is now."

And in walks a twenty-six-year-old buff-handsome jock who also is a convicted rapist. Once Dr. Prendergast leaves the room, Michael is outgoing and polite. The only fuzzy answers are in response to questions about actual events of flashing and raping strangers that have kept him behind razor wires and bars for five years so far. He never mentions his violence toward women. He is equally evasive about date rape.

He says that for *almost* all those sexual experiences, he had a willing partner. I decide to begin at the beginning and ask him about his early years.

AT SEVENTEEN I STARTED FLASHING. IT WAS A THRILL. I'D LOOK FOR LITTLE GIRLS. I WAS INSECURE ABOUT THE SIZE OF MY PENIS.

PUBLIC SCHOOL

WHEN I GOT CAUGHT, ALL I GOT WAS A SLAP ON THE WRIST.

$50.00 FINE AND ONE YEAR PROBATION...

NO BIG DEAL.

I'VE BEEN INSIDE AND IN THERAPY FOR FIVE YEARS. I'M LEARNING ABOUT MYSELF...

MY DAD'S BEATINGS MADE ME FEEL LIKE GARBAGE. TO ME, NOTHING AND NOBODY MATTERED. I COULD HURT ANYBODY. NOW I KNOW I HAVE VALUE.

WHERE IS HE NOW? SINCE THIS INTERVIEW, MICHAEL HAS BEEN RELEASED INTO THE COMMUNITY. NO LAWS ABOUT SEX OFFENDERS REGISTERING WERE IN EFFECT THEN, NO ONE — NOT HIS THERAPIST OR THE PRISON AUTHORITIES — KNOWS WHERE HE IS TODAY, OR WHAT HE IS DOING.

~END~

IDA MARX BLUE SPRUCE

LETTER FROM ELIZABETH

Janet,

Hi. You don't know me, but I had to write. I read your book about rape, and realized I'm **not** the only one. I sure feel like that at times. But I'm at the point where I've got to tell someone.

I'll start at the beginning.

I'm nineteen years old. From the time I was twelve until I was sixteen, my cousin who lived with us raped (that's such a harsh word) and molested me.

Then one year ago I was gang-raped. I thought that because I went to a club I deserved it! I wasn't drinking. I wasn't dressed like a slut. At least I don't think wearing jeans and a sweater means you're one.

Now I feel so violated. They passed me around like I was a bag of chips. I still see the "gang bangers." They live here in the same town. They don't seem to think anything is wrong.

My father's a minister and my mother's a teacher. I did disobey them and went where I shouldn't have. But this seems such a terrible penalty to pay. Anyway, they don't know any of this, and it would kill them if they found out.

Sometimes I feel like ending it all. I can't stand people

standing close to me or certain kinds of cologne. I can still smell their cologne. I still have nightmares.

I wrote my feelings, but not all of them, because I don't want you to judge me. I have no more pride in who I am. Really, what am I? Did I "ask for it?" Will life go on? Will I ever trust people? Will the pain ever go away?

Thanks for writing the book, and for "listening."

Elizabeth,
a Victim

Dear Elizabeth,

You've survived terrible stuff. You should be proud of yourself. When I read your letter, I wanted to remind you of that fact, as well as answer your questions.

Rape is a "harsh" word because what occurs is harsh, horrifying, and dehumanizing. It sears your very soul. No, of course, you didn't "ask for it," and yes, the pain will go away.

But here's the reality: You went through something that won't be forgotten in a month or even a year. Rape does change your life. Still, it doesn't have to stop it.

You've already taken some good steps to begin dealing with what happened. You read a book on the subject. You wrote about it, at least to me. Now you might think about turning to your family and friends for support. You need to stop blaming yourself. You went to a club against your parents' wishes. Testing limits is part of becoming an adult.

You certainly didn't deserve to have such a terrible thing happen as a result. And I have to believe that your parents would find no joy in saying, "We told you so." Look at their jobs. They are both in caring professions. My guess is they would want to protect and help you. No one wants bad things to touch the life of people he or she loves.

I truly understand your hesitance, though. After I was raped, I told my sisters, but especially since my mother had died earlier that year, it took me twelve more months before I let my father know. His reactions? He cried, and he certainly wasn't a man who did that often. He felt guilty for not being able to have kept me from harm's way.

Here's a last point I want to make. What your cousin did to you was made worse by the gang rape. Those experiences combine into such a heavy emotional burden I don't know how you can carry it alone. Please get help, for yourself and in the hope you may be helping others. Your cousin may be molesting more people. If you can't decide how to reach out for guidance, why not talk to a counselor or call a local rape crisis center for advice.

Janet

CHAPTER 9

WHAT KIND OF MAN IS RAPED?

In classrooms when teenagers discuss rape, they talk mainly about a male attacker and a female survivor. In fact, a long-time middle-school teacher, Mark Sherman, says, "Boys have trouble identifying with the problem. Intellectually they understand, but emotionally they can't—or won't—connect."

One in a Hundred

The reality is that men are potential victims, too. Statistics back this up. The Chief of the Manhattan (New York) District Attorney's Sex Crimes Prosecution Unit, Linda Fairstein, reports she has "seen a tremendous increase in the last ten years of violent sexual assaults by male offenders on male victims. And a lot of them are forcible assaults on teenagers."

What about women raping men? "That's a question I'm often asked, especially when I speak to school groups," replies Fairstein. "In my years as a lawyer, although we have had mothers and caretakers of children charged with sexually abusing the kids, I've never had a case of an adult man who charged he was raped by a woman."

Experts estimate that only one in ten women report a sexual assault to the police. For men, the figure is lower: one of every one hundred men sexually assaulted files a formal complaint. New York City Sex Crimes Detective Bruno Francisci adds this detail. "Of the cases we see, about 5 to 10 percent are men. Statistically, though, I think men make up a much larger group."

Men, as well as women, are often trapped by the myths of what kind of man is raped, who rapes him, and the consequences. A member of a Texas rape crisis center, Melinda, says, "In our society there's a big deal about what it is to be a man. If you're raped, sexually abused or molested, so goes the myth, it means you're not tough.

"Real men fight back until they stop it. If you don't, then you're a wimp. Well, that's wrong.

"There's also the belief that if a man's raped by a man, that automatically makes you both homosexual. That's wrong, too. The chances are both the survivor and the perpetrator are heterosexual. Ninety percent of all rapes are committed by straight men.

"Some attack because they want to dominate and humiliate another person, and that man happens to be there. Others are into a con game. They rob a man and know if they rape him as well, the crime is less likely to be reported.

"Still others get involved in gang-rapes. Actually, men are more likely than women to be gang raped and forced into multiple sexual acts. Men are often abused more violently and sustain more injuries. Afterward, to make up for what happened, some male survivors take on this heavy macho way of acting, instead of dealing with feelings."

Beyond that, male or female, the more often you're raped or molested, the closer the relationship to the individual committing the crime, the more devastating the impact.

Adam, now an adult, explains how he came to remember that he had been sexually abused as a child.

In an Age of Consent, Defining Abuse by Adults

. . . Experts on child abuse say [that there are examples where] victims helped foster the abusive relationship and allowed it to continue over time, apparently taking some comfort or pleasure in it.

Although largely unacknowledged, this dynamic is not unusual when sexual abuse involves teenagers—girls as well as boys—instead of prepubescents. It neither justifies nor forgives such relationships, which are forbidden by law for good reason: children under the age of 16, 17, or even 18 are generally not psychologically or emotionally mature enough to consent fully to sexual relationships with adults, or to participate in them on an equal footing.

. . . A heightened sexual curiosity among teenagers could also render them more vulnerable to sexual involvements with adults. Moreover, experts said, limiting the damage done by such involvements and discouraging them in the first place requires a less squeamish discussion about these situations than society is often able to manage.

The New York Times
November 9, 1997
—by Frank Bruni

FINALLY, WE PUT THE WORD OUT IN THE FAMILY, SO OTHER MEMBERS COULD PROTECT THEIR LOVED ONES.

HONEY, DON'T LEAVE THE BABIES ALONE WITH ERIC. HE MOLESTED MY KIDS WHEN THEY WERE SMALL.

THAT'S AWFUL! I'M GLAD YOU WARNED ME.

I THINK DEALING WITH MY MOLESTATION HAS MADE ME A MORE UNDERSTANDING COUNSELOR.

REMEMBER, YOU DIDN'T DO ANYTHING WRONG. YOU'VE GOT TO STOP WHAT'S HAPPENING. THE LONGER IT GOES ON, THE GREATER THE PROBLEMS. DEPRESSION, SUSPICION, VULNERABILITY. TALKING ABOUT THE ABUSE IS THE FIRST STEP TO HEALING.

END

IDA MARX BLUE SPRUCE

Response

CHAPTER 10

IF ONLY
I HADN'T

Across the country, there are psychiatrists, psychologists, and social workers who research issues related to sexual assault and abuse. There are also mental health professionals who take that information and use it to help those whose lives have been touched by this crime. Harriet Lessel, M.S.W., is one of those people.

Her title is Program Coordinator of the Rape Crisis Intervention/Victims of Violence Program, Long Island College Hospital, Brooklyn, New York. Her responsibility is to see rape survivors receive emotional support and understanding.

In addition, Lessel runs groups for teen survivors of these crimes. Here the participants work together to sort through their feelings about their experiences in order to reclaim their lives. And finally, she speaks at schools and to community groups about rape and how attitudes must change.

We meet twice in her office, where the phone rarely stops ringing. When I ask if this job gets to her, she answers, "Absolutely. Sometimes what I hear makes me want to cry. This is personal, too. Rape could happen to me. It's hard to put aside at the end of a day."

We continue the interview with how she defines sexual assault and then go on to what she's learned about it.

Definitions

Sexual assault is *any* unwanted sexual contact. If you're touched in a way that you don't want, that makes you feel uncomfortable—that's sexual assault. So is being forced to look at someone else's body or being forced to show someone else any part of your body. Of course, forced sexual intercourse is rape, too. When the sexual contact is with a family member, we call it incest or molestation.

Dating Rituals

I used to work in a clinic with pregnant teens. I'd say, "Let's talk about your relationship with your boyfriend. How did you get started having sex? What about your ongoing sexual experiences?"

Too often the girls didn't have a good, mutually rewarding sexual relationship. Instead, they had sad stories that fell into the category of rape. But many people believe rape is the victim's fault, and in turn girls are taught to expect the blame for sexual stuff.

Think of the whole dating ritual. Guys are taught to go as far as they can on a date. They don't have to listen to females. Even when a girl is clear, a guy has often been taught to ignore what females say, because, of course, you say no when you mean yes. Or he doesn't care. His wants and desires are what matter.

And then there's the unfair double standard. Parents still are less concerned about their sons' sexual contacts than their daughters'. A lot of girls are raised to be quiet and polite, to not make a scene and to defer to men.

How to change those attitudes and behaviors is a book in itself. At a minimum, you have to realize those traits don't work in today's world. Few of you date only a man or two, and are chaperoned. Few stay home with your parents until you get married. More likely, you have many dating partners. You live independently, at least for a while. Plus now you have to worry about AIDS.

Questions and Messages

There might have been a sexual revolution with increasing numbers supposedly having sex. But the truth is sex means a lot to people. Most don't have the attitude, "I don't care who I do it with."

Today both sexes have to think about the importance of being popular and having dates—and the price. You all have to answer the question, is it better to have a bad steady date than no date at all?

Both sexes have to decide: Do I do it or not? If I have sex, what will it mean? What do I want at this particular time?

The problem is most *adults* feel uncomfortable sitting down with their partners, saying, "Are we ready to have sex?" And you teenagers are just starting out. It's even harder for you to be clear about what you want and don't want; what you think is right and what you think is expected.

So you look around to find messages on how to behave. You still see ads with women used as objects, women in parts —a butt, a breast, a leg—sending the message that women are not people.

Think of movies and TV shows where the man and the woman fight and all of a sudden they're making passionate love. Give me a break! This is not what sex is about. It doesn't happen that way. But these messages help create a climate where rape is acceptable.

The message that *should* go out is that rape is a crime of violence and sex is the weapon.

Trusting Your Instincts

Liana speaks: Parker, a guy in my acting class, asked me to work with him on a scene. It was about a couple arguing about divorce. The method in our program was to immerse yourself in the character. I thought I could get into this role.

Parker found an empty, unlocked room and when we started to read, he kissed me. It didn't fit with the script. I felt uncomfortable. Then he bit my lip until it was bruised and swollen. I wasn't sure what to do. I sort of pushed him away. Still I didn't know, was I being silly? Was he just carried away with his character preparation?

He came onto me again. This time he had a hard-on and started to rub against me. "I have to go," I said, and ran to the girls' room. I started to cry. Why didn't I tell him—stop? Why did I doubt my feelings? I was stupid for thinking I was wrong. What *he* was doing was wrong.

It wasn't an actual rape, but it was abusive. It changed me. And now I found out, a month before with the same scene, he came on to another girl in the same way.

Rape Shock

Everybody thinks date rape is that *he* wants to. *She* doesn't. "Like, forget it; I have a headache tonight." And then he forces her to do it. In reality that is not usually what happens. Often a date rape is planned. There's verbal pressure, maneuvering, and negotiation. The date might be told that someone is home when no one is. Alcohol with or without other drugs may be part of the plan.

In rape both by someone known or unknown, during the actual event you often think you'll be killed. The woman is

71

threatened with death, bodily injury, or harm to a loved one. You feel, "If this guy can rape me, why wouldn't he kill me?" Some women reason, "I'll let him do this so I won't be murdered."

Others are paralyzed by fear. Still others react with a sense of numbness and disbelief, feeling—it can't be happening to me. The rape is so overwhelming that the only thing the mind can do is say *no*.

After you've been raped, you experience different reactions. We call it the Rape Trauma Syndrome, the survivor's short- and long-term response to this terrible event. Right afterwards, many survivors are still in shock. You might feel afraid, embarrassed, dirty, guilty, and ashamed. And most people blame themselves.

You think you did something to bring this on: "If I hadn't been hanging out with those people." "If I hadn't worn that." "If I hadn't said that." "If I hadn't smoked dope."

I say to people over and over, "It's not your fault. It is the fault of the person who did this to you."

The only thing you might have done is not use good judgment. Or you might have gotten yourself into a situation where your senses are telling you, I'm uncomfortable, but you don't want to make a scene. You want to be cool, because maybe you want to be with this guy and you don't think anything is ever going to happen. Until it does. And remember, if a guy rapes once, he'll probably do it again.

Twist of the Knife

Everyone expresses distress and stress through his or her body. During this first phase after the rape you might have physical problems. Headaches. Stomachaches. Insomnia. Lack of appetite. You might feel achy not only in the parts of your body that were attacked, but in other places as well. At the same time, depending on the individual, you could also feel anxious, nervous, talkative, or super quiet.

Some react by thinking, "Well, it happened two weeks ago . . . it happened two months ago. I'm fine." That's unrealistic. You have to allow yourself time to heal, and most people don't do that. You think it's over, because you want to put it behind you. You don't want to understand that it is going to continue to affect you for a long time.

These short-term reactions can last anywhere from about four to eight weeks.

During the long-term phase, you start to deal with feelings and reorganizing your life. This is when nightmares might start. This is your mind's way of coping with the trauma.

While you begin to resume your normal activities, you may want to change your routine. For example, you change the way you walk to school. Or you don't go anywhere alone. Maybe you want to move away . . . change your phone number . . . analyze your life to ensure your safety.

Inside you there are changes, too. You feel overwhelmed emotionally. The only way you'll rid yourself of these demons is to handle them little by little. You'll never forget being raped. But the twist of the knife—the worst feelings—go away. They won't, however, go away quickly.

You'll start to understand these feelings are the result of the rape. Let's say you're anxious about going back to school. Why? You have to face the person who did it. Now you know the source of your feelings. Then you can make up your mind that today you're not going to school. Or you understand where these feelings are coming from, but you're going to school anyway.

You can't ignore these feelings. They don't just vanish. They come out in other ways. Maybe, for instance, you start fighting with your family. What's happening is you weren't allowed to express anger during the rape. Now, though, you feel safe expressing it.

You may worry about sexuality and having a happy sex life. Remember rape is not sex. A mutual, caring sexual relationship is 180 degrees different from a rape. Rape is a loss of control. It is violence. A penis has been used as the weapon. It is not two people making love.

Starting Over

For virgins, it's particularly difficult. Women have a lot of feelings about the first time they have a sexual relationship. But you did not want the rape to happen. You didn't willingly give yourself. At the same time, though, you have to grieve the loss of your virginity.

Starting a sexual relationship or resuming one *is* hard. You may not feel sexual desire. When you have sex, you may find yourself in a position that reminds you of the rape. Even if you are in a good relationship, it's normal to take a long time to feel comfortable with the sexual part.

If the boyfriend knows about the rape, many immediately want to have sex again. It's, like, "Well, come on, we had a good thing going. Let's do it."

And you may want to prove to yourself that, yes, you can have good sex. Still, be clear; if you don't want sex, don't do it. Especially when you've been raped by someone you know, loss of trust and what that means in future relationships is more extensive than when the rape was by a stranger.

Step back to square one and go with your instincts. You need to feel good enough to be assertive about who you want to touch your body and when. It takes time to develop a loving sexual relationship, but *time does heal*.

If you feel depressed, however, go for extra help. It does not mean you're crazy. It's the sanest thing to do. You are reacting to a life-threatening experience that has thrown you topsy-turvy. Talk to a trusted friend or adult, a school counselor, a therapist, a nurse, or pick up the phone directory and find a rape crisis center. (See Chapter 12.)

How should you react if you learn a loved one has been raped?

Lessel: Immediately show your support. Because rape removes a person's control, help the survivor start to regain control over her life.

I can't give you the words, but if she wants to, encourage her to talk about the incident. You don't want the details. Rather you want to make sure she's okay. How is she feeling? Has she been checked medically? Does she want to do that? Has she told anybody else?

She's gone through a traumatic event. Remind her, she's survived! If she starts to blame herself, "Maybe I should have done this and that," say, "But you're alive. Whatever you did was right because here you are. I'm proud of you. You can get the help you want, and I'll help you do that in any way I can."

Remember, too, a rape is unwanted sexual contact. Don't rush over and throw your arms around her. She might not want it. If you can't sense whether it's okay, ask. How people treat the survivor means a lot in terms of recovery. Be respectful of what she's told you; do not tell others.

Reaching Out

Many rape survivors never tell anybody what happened. I encourage you to tell someone. It makes you feel better. Carrying the burden of a rape by yourself is too hard.

Some of you don't want to tell your parents. "We don't have a good relationship," you say. "They'll blame me. It's one more problem we'll have with each other." But many have been surprised by their parents' supportive reactions.

There's no magic way to tell them so they won't get upset. Just say to whichever parent you feel is best, "I have something important to tell you. I need your help." That's why you're doing it. You need their advice.

Sometimes family members flip out and yell at you. They rant and rave, "I'll kill that rapist!" That's not helpful to you, but that's how they deal with their own feelings. Other times they want you to report the rape and you don't want to. Then it becomes a power issue, when the final decision, I feel, should be with the survivor. You might tell them, "I need your love and concern, not your anger and your I-told-you-so."

Telling friends isn't always easy, either. If it's a friend you trust, chances are that person will be supportive. But sometimes even people you love make mistakes in their reaction. They don't know better.

Rape is such a fearful thing that people distance themselves from it by blaming the victim. They think, "She did such and such. That's why she was raped. I would never do that, so I can't be raped."

Because of the myths, some boyfriends, like some parents and some girlfriends, can't handle the information. They think in some way you were at fault.

Other guys feel disgusted with a woman after a rape. They think of a female as property—now spoiled. But you know what? If your boyfriend thinks that, dump him. If you've been in a loving relationship, it's tough to drop him. But he'll end up making you feel worse, and that's the last thing you need.

While you're recovering from a rape, *you* have to be the

most important person in your life: not your boyfriend, not your parents, not the rest of your family, not your friends. If people are not supportive, don't talk to them. If they make you feel bad, say, "I'm not having this conversation anymore."

Time

Any person who has been raped can get better. You can take back power and control over your life. And even though this sounds weird, having something like this happen in your life can make you evaluate many other things. You can take a dev-

Apple's Way
SONGWRITING HELPED FIONA APPLE SPEAK OF THE UNSPEAKABLE

... 19 year-old Fiona Apple, then 12, was raped by an intruder in the apartment building where she lived with her mother and sister. ... Already a melancholy and withdrawn child, Apple says she had a hard time communicating her feelings of violation and anger. "I got sick and tired of going to my parents, my teachers, my friends and shrinks and telling them how I felt about things and feeling totally misunderstood," she says.

Apple began pouring her feelings into songs. ... "We learn from our pain," she says. "It enriches life. ..." Now her album is steadily climbing the *Billboard* album chart ... her video is getting heavy airplay on MTV and VH1. ...

People
November 25, 1996
—by Jeremy Helligar

astating experience, turn it around and make positive things come out of it. There's a chance for real personal growth.

All it takes is time.

Where Is Harriet Lessel Now? Today the project Harriet Lessel coordinates has changed its name to reflect its expanded goal: to meet the needs of adults who were sexually abused as children, as well as survivors of domestic violence and other crimes. The project is now called the Rape Crisis Intervention/Victims of Violence Program.

"In the past, victim services were not geared specifically to teens," says Lessel. "Teens didn't use them much, despite high rates of rape. Now our program and other rape crisis programs nationwide are increasingly recognizing teen rights. And we need to, because teen versus teen violence, including sexual violence, is an increasing problem. However, what's changing is that schools are better prepared to put the rights of the survivor before those of the perpetrator."

She also stresses the dangers of the so-called date rape drugs, Rohypnol and GHB, Liquid X. A few years ago, they were practically unknown. Now, says Lessel, they are seeing young women who have been drugged and sexually assaulted.

These drugs make it easier for rapists to commit their crimes. They don't have to use force. They don't have to threaten harm, subdue the victim, or worry about screams. And afterward, because the survivors have no memories, the chances of prosecution are far more difficult. In fact, often their stories are not believed.

CHAPTER *11*

LETTER FROM AMY

Dear Janet

I was helping my daughter clean her room when I came across your book. When I was around 8 my dad started to do things with me—a lot more than touching. Right from the start, I kinda knew it was wrong. As I grew older, I tried to avoid him. Going anywhere alone with him was scary.

Once he took me fishing. He held me over his head and threatened to throw me in the river if I didn't do stuff with him. Being a kid, I believed him.

Then he wanted me to go on a hike with him. My mom said, go with your dad. About 30 seconds passed. I looked to my dad then to my mom. Back and forth. We were taught to obey our parents. I had to go. But, thank god for curiosity. My brother shadowed us up the hill. He saw what my dad did to me.

He was shocked. He ran home and told mom. That night she let me know what he saw. For once I had her complete love and understanding. Never to be repeated.

Hell broke loose after that day. My mom turned my dad in. I was taken to the hospital. It was terrifying.

The result of all this: my dad was in jail for one week. He was supposed to go to a clinic for help, but wasn't really forced to. I was never taken out of the home. Why not? Why not? Why was I left to face it all on my own, I wondered.

My mom said for me and my brothers (I have an older one, too) never to say anything to anybody about what happened. So that's what we did. Life went on just like nothing took place. But it did.

I still have all the memories like it was yesterday.

When I started going out with guys, my father believed if I could kiss and let them hug me, he could, too. He never left me alone. I'd block the door to my bedroom so he couldn't get in. I tried not to leave it unless I was sure someone else was around.

At 16 I got pregnant and married to get out of the house. Today I'm 31 and it was my now-teenage daughter reading your book.

My dad's getting older. I'm not gonna ever trust him or believe he's cured of his sickness. I often wonder how different my life would have been if none of this had ever happened. Of course, I'll never know. I only know I survived because I wanted to. I tried lots of ways to overcome it all. But nobody helped me. No one whatsoever. Just myself.

Amy

Dear Amy,

It's bad enough to be raped once by a stranger or a date from school. But when the person raping you over and over is a family member, a person you know and trust and may even love, the emotional fall out touches many additional parts of your life. Of course, you know that.

Incest is so much more complicated an issue, it's a book in itself. *Voices of Rape* is a place to start, before you look further for more information and help.

You sound like a courageous woman, a determined survivor. I'm glad you seem to be succeeding in taking charge of your life. But Amy, I'm not a therapist, I'm a writer. If you haven't done it, you might want to get some counseling for yourself and advice about your daughter. Why exactly did she have my book? What's going on in her life? Has she ever been left alone with your dad? From your letter, I can see why you don't trust him. It could be justified.

Janet

CHAPTER 12

IT COULD BE THE MOST IMPORTANT CALL YOU MAKE

There are hundreds of rape crisis centers nationwide. Some are in hospitals, others out in the community. With hospital programs, an advocate—kind of an emotional helper and resource person—is called if you seek medical care at that particular facility after a rape. (See Chapters 10 and 16.)

Remove the Mystery

With community programs, you make the call. But it could be the most important call you make. Whether you, a friend, or a family member were sexually assaulted minutes or a lifetime ago, advocates are available to give callers emotional support and practical information.

Maybe you wonder, "Should I report the attack to the police?" Counselors at the centers won't tell you yes or no. Instead, they explain why it's best you make the decision. To help you, though, they remove the mystery: they tell you what to expect if you dial 911.

Do you think, as a result of the rape, you might have gotten a sexually transmitted disease (STD), including AIDS? Advocates give you names and numbers of places where you can receive free, confidential testing.

Maybe after becoming sexually active, you start having flashbacks to when you were molested as a child. Together, you and an advocate decide how best today to handle that past situation.

Rape-crisis-center advocates answer your questions, even those you didn't know you had. They help you realize you are not alone. They believe in you.

In addition, some centers run personal-safety classes. Others sponsor teen theater groups that put on performances about topics related to sexual assault. Still others lobby state legislatures to improve rape laws. And ultimately, they help you understand how to go about reclaiming your life.

Local and National Help

To find the telephone number for a local center, check your directory white pages. Look in the front of the book under Emergency Numbers, in the alphabetical listings under Women Against Rape or Rape Intervention Program /Hotline/Counseling, or dial "O" and ask the operator for assistance.

If your questions are still unanswered, try any of the organizations listed on the following pages. Be patient. Many numbers are answered first by machines. You may be asked to press 1 to speak to a counselor, press 2 for brochures, and so on.

Be cautious. When doing any Web or Internet searches on this issue, be aware that you might come across virtual vi-

olence against women. For a comprehensive listing of women's organizations by state, start with:
http://www.feminist.org/911/resources.html
    For health advice and information, try **Go Ask Alice**:
http://kwaziwai.cc.columbia.edu/cu/healthwise/alice.html

Childhelp USA/National Child Abuse Hotline
800/4-A-CHILD
National Office
15757 N. 78th Street
Scottsdale, AZ 85260
602/922-8212
http://www.childhelpusa.org

    East Coast Regional Office
    120 N. Lee Street
    Falls Church, VA 22046
    703/241-9100

    LA Regional Office
    1345 El Centro Avenue
    Hollywood, CA 90028
    213/465-4016

    Tennessee Office
    2505 Kingston Road
    Knoxville, TN 37913
    423/637-1753

National Coalition Against Sexual Assault
P.O. Box 21378
Washington, DC 20009
202/483-7165

National Clearinghouse on Marital and Date Rape
510/524-1582
http://members.aol.com/ncmdr/index.html

National Organization for Victim Assistance
202/232-6682
http://www.access.digex.net/~nova
nova@access.digex.net

National Victim Center
2111 Wilson Boulevard
#300
Arlington, VA 22201
703/276-2880
NVC@mail.nvc.org

National Youth Crisis Hotline
800/448-4663
http://www.ydi.org

RAINN: Rape, Abuse, Incest National Network
800/656-HOPE (4673)
http://www.rainn.org

Sexual Assault Crisis Center
P.O. Box 1207
Meridian, MS 39302
800/643-6250

**The Kempe National Center for the Prevention and
    Treatment of Child Abuse and Neglect**
The National Adolescent Perpetrator Network
1205 Oneida Street

Denver, CO 80222
303/321-3963

(Contact information varies according to the organization. At present, not all have Web sites or e-mail addresses. Some only want phone calls or snail mail.)

TECHNO.FEM
Cyber-Rape: How Virtual Is It?

. . . No doubt, the Internet makes it easier for disturbed people to find each other or to identify unwitting victims. Participants' risk of being victimized is being heightened by the fact that the Internet also encourages a false sense of trust and of what's real and what's make-believe. A person can omit certain facts about themselves, or accentuate the qualities that might be more socially acceptable—so even the most unbalanced person might appear sane on-line. . . .

Given that more women are going on-line, the prevalence of graphic depictions of sexual violence will bring pornography into an increasing number of women's lives. . . .

What does all this bode for the future? There have already been cases where sexual violence on-line has reached beyond the keyboard. It seems inevitable that more such cases will occur. And there is no doubt that new technology will also reshape on-line interactions. . . .

Groups of women together can chase violators out of chat rooms by simply barraging the interloper with "get lost" messages. We can also insist that Internet providers prevent users from changing their on-line names and profiles at will. While users could remain anonymous, by making them stick to one name, a degree of accountability would be instituted. You wouldn't be able to behave abusively under one name and then take another one to hide behind. . . .

Ms.
March/April 1997
—by Debra Michals

CHAPTER 13

NICE BOYS CAN DO BAD THINGS

When Judith V. Becker was studying for her Ph.D., a supervisor was doing pioneer research in sexual deviance and adult sex offenders. He asked, would she like to help? She agreed.

Now, two decades later, Dr. Becker is an expert with an international reputation for her work with juvenile sex offenders. The morning we meet, her desk is covered with articles, books, and at least fifteen orange slips of paper—telephone messages. The day before she'd been on television and was quoted on the front page of the *New York Times*.

She says it seems as if everybody just realized that teenagers rape, and not only minority teens from troubled backgrounds. White teens—popular, good-looking guys, stars of their middle-class and upper-class high schools—can rape, too. During our discussion, we first look at why Dr. Becker focused on juvenile sex offenders, and what she has learned in the process.

—— **JUDITH V. BECKER, Ph.D.** ——

Peeping Toms and Exhibitionists

Back when my supervisor and I worked with adult sex offenders, we learned that 60 percent had started committing the crimes when they were juveniles. And they had committed hundreds if not thousands of sexual crimes during their lifetime. We also learned that they can have what we call a deviant sexual-interest pattern. I'll explain that.

Years ago, the belief was that peeping toms were just peeping toms. We didn't have to worry they'd do anything else. Exhibitionists? They were just shy. Showing us their penis was their way of asking for a date.

Well, those beliefs were wrong. For example, half of these "shy" exhibitionists had fantasies about or had engaged in sexual acts with children. About 20 percent of them had fantasies about or had raped adults.

We also learned to be concerned about young boys with the following kinds of behavior:

Red Alert—Beware If Young Boys . . .

- Make obscene phone calls
- Engage in voyeuristic (peeping tom) behavior
- Show their penis to somebody
- Mistreat animals
- Dress up in women's clothing
- Stalk and humiliate their classmates
- Rehearse assaults

We even had examples of boys acting out assaults with their teddy bears. Often people write it off as "boys being boys," and in some cases, it may be. In other cases, however, this is the start. It leads to more serious sexual crimes.

More Danger Signs

Now I'm talking more directly to the male readers. Think of the behaviors I mentioned this way. Some of you kids take a drink or smoke a joint at ages eight, nine, or ten. Not all of you become alcoholics or go on to mainline drugs. But a certain percentage of you will, and you should be concerned if you think you might be part of that percentage.

Thoughts—in this case, your sexual thoughts—are much harder to uncover. If you have thoughts involving sex with relatives—if you think about doing sexual things with a brother, sister, mother, whoever—you need to be concerned. If you have thoughts about *forcing* sex on someone, you need to be concerned. If you like seeing people being hurt, injured, or shamed, you need to be concerned about that, too.

Most importantly, you should never masturbate to any of those thoughts. The masturbation reinforces the behavior. What people think about sexually and what they reinforce through masturbation can be a rehearsal for the actual deviant behavior.

If you behave this way or have these kinds of sexual thoughts, you're not a bad person. It just means you need help. Find a trusted adult to put you in contact with programs that deal with these problems.

Curiosity

You kids *are* curious about sex. It's normal to feel aroused by or attracted to people. Sex can be healthy behavior when engaged in responsibly and at an age when you are aware of the risks and the benefits.

But normal sexual curiosity and behavior involves two people of the same age, both agreeing to do something. There's no threat. No bribe.

Curiosity is not a fifteen-year-old and a five-year-old. Curiosity is not two seven-year-olds where one is holding a stick and saying, "Show me your vagina or I'll hit you." Curiosity is not two people of the same age, one with an IQ of 120 and the other with an IQ of 50.

I'm a researcher. While I don't have the data to support it, my sense is there's an increase in deviant sexual behavior among teenagers. One reason I think we're in such a mess now is that adults are not open to your curiosity about sex. Adults don't want to talk about it.

On the nightly news, though, there are routine reports about sexual assault. Even little kids watching TV can hear about things like gang rape. Television allows you to learn about sexual misuse when you haven't yet learned about healthy sexuality.

Violent Nation

We're a violent society that objectifies women. Consequently, we have a higher rate of rape than other countries. And the states within our nation with the highest rates have widespread approval of what we might call legitimate violence—the death penalty, few restrictions on carrying guns, and residents who are into violent contact sports, such as football.

On the other hand, in the Scandinavian countries, for example, there are laws against the death penalty, carrying guns, and so on, as well as much more openness about sexuality. As a result, the rape rates are much lower. In our country, we think if adults talk to kids about sex, you're going to go out and be sexual. There are no data, however, to support that.

More and more of you are growing up in families where you see parents bring multiple partners into the home. You're not being parented. You're being left alone to abuse your peers, and you are being placed in the role of baby-sitter, where you can initiate younger kids into sex. In addition, many of you are being abused by a parent, a sibling, or a next-door neighbor.

We must be concerned about the abused becoming the abuser. We know that sexually abused boys are at greater risk of becoming abusers themselves. In fact, 40 percent of sex offenders have been sexually abused. Sixty percent were physically abused.

When I say "sexually abused," I've heard of every type of act imaginable: sexual intercourse, masturbating, being masturbated, oral sex, foreign objects being inserted into the anus, fondling, and so on.

Bad Luck

Initially when we started to work with juvenile sex offenders, we asked them, "Have you ever been sexually abused?" We realized, however, it's difficult to admit that. So we began to say, "We'd like you to tell us about every person with whom you've had a sexual experience."

And then we ask, "How old were you?" "How old was the other person?" "Was this person a relative?" "Was this other person male or female?" With that last question, we found that boys are less likely to disclose sexual contact they've had with a woman. Yet when we say, "Did you initiate the behavior?" the answer is no.

"Do you define that as sexual abuse?" we ask them.

"No."

"Why not?"

"Well, boys are supposed to feel lucky if a woman has sex with them."

"If a man did that to you, would it be sexual abuse?" we ask.

"Yes."

Some sexually abused boys act it out either sexually against other people or their overall aggressive behavior may increase. But not all do that. They develop empathy because they have been the victim. They never do anything like that to other people.

We also know that sexually abused girls internalize their pain. They turn it in against themselves. In other words, girls usually develop anxiety disorders. They may get depressed. If they act it out, they may become sexually promiscuous.

THE CYCLE

Peggy Greene, a Maryland Juvenile Correctional Consultant, speaks about her experiences in her work with sexually abused adolescents:

I think of Jenny telling me how her stepdad constantly abused her and her sister. Their mom often participated. The sad thing is these sisters thought it was normal.

I think of another family, two brothers, Raymond and Connor. Not only were they sexually abused, but also they were burned with cigarettes by their mother's boyfriends. I remember reading their file and crying.

Then there's Becca. After six months of therapy, she agrees to confront her abusive father and tell her mom about the molesting. When she does, the volcano erupts. Mom screams, "How could you say such a thing," and goes to slap Becca. The therapist intervenes. The father calls Becca a whore. She's sobbing, saying, "Mom, you've known all along." I take Becca out of the room. Mom and Dad walk out the door, still screaming, and drive away.

(I want to yell, too, but back at all those adults, "You filthy scum trash. Getting your thrills by taking advantage of vulnerable kids." But I have to be "therapeutic" and mask the horror I feel.)

We have to try to get through to these kids. It's tough. They put up walls to hide behind so no one and nothing else can hurt them. And too often while hiding, they contrive how to get even. They trap themselves in the cycle. The abused become the abusers.

Unmailed Letters

In some sex offender groups, the offender has to post a list in his room of all his victims. In group sessions he has to call out their names. He has to write and read unmailed letters to the victims. The goal is to help him see the victim is a person.

We have to make these kids *feel*. We have to dig deep and get inside. We have to get the whole family involved. It's possible, but it takes time. The way our social service system is overloaded, we must hurry to get them in and out to make room for the ton more waiting for help. Too often they show up next in juvenile detention centers, boot camps, and prisons.

In her own way Jenny stopped the cycle of abuse by giving up the baby she had to adoption. Raymond has become a "fire bug," burning everything in sight. Connor swings between being withdrawn and volatile. Becca went to live with a cousin and remains in therapy.

Mixed Group

Rapists are a mixed group. Their motivation varies. However, some individuals—we call them antisocial—do not care about other people's feelings. They have no sense of right and wrong. These people rob, maim, and rape. They commit what are known as crimes of opportunity.

Say a man breaks into an apartment to take the money, the TV, and the VCR. Unknown to him, a woman's sleeping in the next room. He sees her and thinks, "As long as I'm here, I might as well rape her." So he does.

Some individuals are only turned on by violent sex. They

may have a girlfriend, they may be married. But when the person agrees to sex, it's not erotic—not sexy—to them.

Others aren't severely mentally ill, but they are intellectually limited. They may be twenty-year-olds but have the mental age of a ten-year-old. Because they are more comfortable around ten-year-olds, maybe they sexualize the relationship.

Still others are severely mentally ill or have something wrong with part of their brain. They have trouble controlling their thinking and their general behavior. They see someone, feel an attraction, and act on that feeling by forcing sex on that person.

Date Rape

Teenagers are more likely to run into these kinds of situations: under the influence of alcohol or drugs—which we know affects our ability to control our behavior—you do things you wouldn't normally do, including rape.

That's not an excuse for the behavior. It's what happens and it means you should stay away from those things.

When males get together, some feel a way of asserting or proving their masculinity is by showing how macho they are. A way to do that is by having sex—all of them raping one girl.

The fact is that rape is not an expression of masculinity. It's an expression of cowardice. Anyone sure of himself doesn't have to engage in a cowardly act by forcing sex on another person—particularly when the odds are so much in the gang's favor.

Still other individuals prefer to have sex with a peer and prefer to have consensual sex—sex that both people agree to. But when that person isn't available, or that person says no, then they force sex on either that person or another person. A lot of date rapes fall into this category.

Boys need to know that when a girl says no, you respect

that no. And girls need to know that if you mean no, you should say no. If you mean yes, you should say yes. However, if you say yes to some things but no to other things, you have to be clear.

Sexual behavior starts with looking at someone you find attractive. The next step is wanting that person to notice you. Maybe after that, you go out. You want to touch that person.

Montana Law to Allow Injections for Rapists

... Hoping to save money on prisons, Montana has become the second state to approve the use of "chemical castration" to reduce the sexual drive of sexual offenders who are about to be released from prison.

A similar program went into effect this year in California where the law mandates that offenders convicted of child molestation for a second time be injected with a drug, usually Depo-Provera, that reduces testosterone levels, which in return reduces sexual drive. ...

... Although the new law has broad support and the treatment is widely used in Europe, some people have questioned the use of such methods. "It's a simplistic, feel-good piece of legislation that doesn't get at the root of the problem," said Scott Crichton, executive director of the American Civil Liberties Union of Montana.

The New York Times
April 27, 1997
—by *The New York Times*

But you need the person's permission. So maybe you kiss, but again you need the other person's permission to kiss.

After that, maybe you want to do some upper-body touching. Still, though, you need the other person's permission. Next might be that you want some genital touching. Once again you need permission.

The person can give permission anywhere along the line. But at a critical point, permission might not be granted for whatever reason—sexually transmitted diseases, fear of pregnancy, the girl wants to wait until she is an adult in a committed relationship.

Boys need to be prepared to stop anywhere in that process. Girls have to be prepared to say no and to mean it. When a girl says, "No, no, no . . . well, okay," the boy is confused. And I am in no way holding girls responsible for being assaulted or the victims of date rape.

Power to Humiliate

Men rape because it makes them feel powerful. They want to humiliate the other person. Most importantly, they are aroused by the behavior. They get erections. Sometimes, but not always, they ejaculate.

Some people say there's nothing sexual about rape; that rape is purely violence. That's not true. It's sex and violence. At sexual behavior clinics, we treat adolescents between the ages of thirteen and eighteen who have misused their sexuality.

Lots of people see them as scum and say, "We should execute them." Others say, "No, we should castrate them." Studies have been done on castrating individuals. First of all, we can remove a person's testicles and they still get erections. Remove the penis, too? A person doesn't need a penis to molest someone. He still has his hands, his mouth, foreign objects. So that's not going to solve the problem.

Lock up the person? Yes, that would stop them from committing sexual crimes for as long as they're in jail. But most people eventually get out, and when they do they start all over again. Jail is not the solution.

Yesterday I was on TV. People wanted to know how nice kids could rape. I said, "Unfortunately, nice boys can do bad things." People don't buy that. They think if you do something bad, you're a bad person. The fact is there are nice people who do horrible things. But you don't throw away the person. You try to change the behavior. That's where clinics come in.

Clinics vary, but programs often offer outpatient treatment free of charge. Youngsters are evaluated so we can see what their needs and strengths are. Initially, the therapy is individual and then they are moved into groups. Because most kids deny or minimize what they did, one goal is to help them accept full responsibility.

In the process we want to know how they gave themselves permission to do what they did. How did they justify the behavior? Then we challenge that and try to give them other ways of looking at situations and at their actions.

We also look at risky situations to them, the early warning signs to their behavior. We teach them how to avoid those situations. We teach them the effects of their behavior on their victims and how this can continue for the rest of the victims' lives.

Then we help them develop the skills to maintain good relationships with their peers. Because we're taking something away, we must make sure they know how to have future relationships that are good ones.

But we're like an oasis. They come here and we try to undo a lot of what society has done. When the boys leave, we pray to God that they will maintain what they've learned. The truth? They won't find a whole lot of reinforcement out there.

Where Is Judith Becker Now? Judith Becker left New York City and is now at the University of Arizona, where she is the Associate Dean for Academic Affairs for Social and Behavioral Sciences and a professor of psychology and psychiatry.

In a follow-up phone call, she said a major change she sees is that many states are now looking at registering adolescent sexual offenders, as well as notifying community members if ex-sex offenders move into their neighborhoods.

This troubles her. "It's fine for police departments to know who the youthful offenders are," she says. However, Dr. Becker has some doubts about providing the general public with this information. "People need to take a judicious approach to this," she cautions.

Report

CHAPTER 14

THE POLICE DON'T WANT THIS TO CONTINUE

Whether to report a sexual assault to the police is generally up to the survivor. Although the number of date and acquaintance rapes brought to the police's attention is increasing, rapes committed by strangers and those with significant physical violence are still more likely to wind up on police blotters.

To find out what happens if you do report, I talk with Detective Bruno Francisci of the Manhattan Sex Crimes Squad. His station is on a tree-lined residential street, but inside it's police business as usual: criminals and victims, interrogations and two-way mirrors.

Before the interview, Detective Francisci flips the switch on a tape recorder. For the next fifteen minutes, I listen to him question a teenage male accused of sexually abusing a five-year-old girl.

On the recording, after introducing himself, Detective Francisci asks the teenager his name, date of birth, and address. Then he advises him of his rights, letting him know he can request the presence of a lawyer. After a brief hesitation, the teenager says, "I'll answer the questions."

In a low-keyed manner, the detective and the accused move through the telling and retelling of the event. With each retelling, the detective uncovers new details of what the teenager says took place.

Detective Francisci comes from a big family. When he handles these investigations, he admits there are times he can't help but think of those closest to him. In this police-eye-view of sexual assault, we first discuss how rape survivors differ from other crime victims.

—— DETECTIVE BRUNO FRANCISCI ——

Bogeymen

Victims of sexual assault have to be handled much differently than, say, a person whose car was vandalized. They often feel responsible, "If I didn't take that shortcut to get home, I wouldn't have been attacked."

Or a daughter might say, "If I didn't come out of the bathroom with a towel wrapped around me, my father wouldn't have abused me."

We try to defuse the victim's feelings of guilt. Like, we have a thirteen-year-old who's been repeatedly raped by her cousin. He started abusing the girl when she was young, and she didn't know they were doing anything wrong. He'd say, "It's done all the time."

As she gets older, there's talk about child abuse in school. All of a sudden she thinks, "Hey, this is not an appropriate action for a cousin." When it comes to light, we investigate.

What do we do?

This teenager is in a dilemma. To her, the police are the bogeymen who are going to put her cousin in jail. She's never going to see him again. No matter what that guy has done to her, there may still be a strong family bond.

We have to compile information, but the first step is to break the ice and win the trust of the victim. We're not the bad guys. And what the attacker has done is not acceptable.

We explain, "Look, you did nothing wrong. Our objective is to help you and your family. We don't want this to continue." See, we also know that many people who sexually abuse kids at some point let that child go and start on a younger child.

Two-Unknown-People

Let's back up now to what happens if the person is a victim of a "traditional" rape: the two-unknown-people type of situation. The first thing the victim should do is call 911 and give as accurate a description of the individual as possible.

This man is now fleeing. There's a chance that with a description somebody may come across him, and he can be apprehended by the police.

The department tries to limit how involved the uniformed officers who first respond get with the victim. They haven't received the extra training on handling these cases that those in the Sex Crimes Squad have. So in the academy, they are taught to limit their questions. In twenty-five words or less, try to find out what happened.

Maybe some guy grabbed you from behind at knifepoint and subsequently raped you. End of story. The officers call the Sex Crimes Squad and we take over.

Sometimes the victim doesn't want to have further police contact or has second thoughts after calling them, like, "I don't really want to do this." In that case, we have the uniformed officers back off. Then, depending on the circumstances, we might wait until the next morning or afternoon to call. But at some point, we speak to the victim.

Down the Drain

If the assault happens in your home, leave the room exactly as it was. There's a tendency to clean up. The feeling, "Oh, I'm getting company," for lack of a better way to put it.

By cleaning, a woman destroys a lot of evidence.

Same thing with clothes. We've gotten to the scene and the washing machine is going. All the evidence is going down the drain. Don't touch anything. As a person, I understand the victim wants to erase it all. But for the police to do an investigation, having little evidence is a problem.

Next a victim should get medical attention. We can send an ambulance, a car, or you can see your own doctor. But if you go to a hospital, there are often crisis intervention people to assist you. Again, I know you might not want to go to the hospital. Strictly from the investigator's point of view, there's evidence to be gathered. If nothing else, it's a preventive measure against venereal disease. In any case, I feel the victim should go.

Okay, so you've told the story to the uniformed officers, gone to the hospital, and let's say it's one-thirty in the morning. We give the person options, which is another important facet of this investigation. A victim of rape has lost all the control. The rapist orders you: "Take this off. Put this on."

Right away we try to give you back a feeling of control. We know, for example, certain hospitals are hectic. You may have to be there for two, three hours, being poked and prodded. So we might say, "Look, we'll come to your house tomorrow. Is that good for you? Or would you rather talk to us now?" You make the decision, and we get you when you're more at ease, more aware of what transpired.

Reno Launches Drive Against "Date Rape Drugs"

Safety: Campaign will explain the dangers to students, U.S. attorney general says

. . . Atty. Gen. Janet Reno outlined a campaign to flood college campuses with posters and other written information explaining the dangers of the drugs—Rohypnol and GHB—and to air public service announcements.

. . . Reno's appearance underscored the breadth of a problem that is frustrating police, hospitals and rape victims. . . . Many investigators and laboratories are still struggling to understand, trace and prosecute crimes—particularly sexual assaults—involving these drugs' use.

. . . Victims must report the crime and seek medical treatment immediately, because the drugs can leave the system within hours. Even then, victims may wind up dealing with doctors or investigators unfamiliar with the drugs.

. . . After reviewing their investigative techniques late last year, the Los Angeles Police Department and Los Angeles County Sheriff Department decided to seek urine samples from rape victims because traces of Rohypnol and GHB are evident longer in urine than blood. Investigators are also being trained to look for evidence of the substances—residue on glasses, leftover drinks—at the crime scene. . . .

The Los Angeles Times
August 12, 1997
—by Jeff Leeds

Forthright and Truthful

To make the victim more comfortable, I'm not in uniform. When we meet, I usually take off my gun and 'cuffs. I introduce myself: "My name is Bruno. I'm with the police department. We're here to talk to you."

There's no set repertoire. Each case is different. We don't, though, go right into the subject matter, the allegation. People tend to get uptight with the police. I want you, the person I'm talking to, to understand I'm on your side.

Maybe we'll spend fifteen, twenty minutes, shooting the breeze. We'll talk about your family, where you go to school. Then we'll come around to the assault.

I let you tell me what happened at your own pace. After you say it once and the roof hasn't fallen in, you realize you can go back and get more specific. If you have difficulty talking about what happened, we have dolls you can use to act it out.

We use this method frequently with little kids. We go through the scenario with limited conversation. We don't pressure the victims. In fact, sometimes if we realize there is difficulty, we stop.

And, by the way, a female officer is available, if that's what you prefer. There is also a certain amount of confidentiality. Don't worry about me discussing this with your parents. Although they are involved as parents, there's no reason for them to have the details.

A victim is sometimes skeptical whether I'm going to believe what you're telling me. I immediately reassure you, "We're not here to doubt what happened. We're here to get the facts. You were the victim of a crime. We didn't want this to happen to you in the first place, let alone anyone else in the future."

We want the victim to be forthright and truthful. If you

don't tell us something, for example, you were doing drugs, and the people we arrest tell us about it, there's a problem.

But as far as we're concerned, even if you do drugs every day, no one has the right to force themselves on you and to use you like a piece of property.

Or say I'm interviewing you again. I look over the police report and see that the hospital gynecologist says you have certain injuries and oh, by the way, you're pregnant. I need to ask you about it.

We need to know if you know who is the father of the child—even if it's the guy who raped you last night. In your mind the fact that you're pregnant, might mean we think, "Oh, she's sleeping with everybody in town." But being pregnant has nothing to do with being raped. We have to know what's what to build a strong case.

Pattern Guys

The next step is to show you our parolee photos, pictures of men who've already served time in jail for sexual assault. These are what we usually call "pattern guys." That is to say, we get three or four different incidents that have a connection to a single attacker. There's a certain way the guy does it each time.

When we start seeing that, what comes to our mind is a parolee—a sex offender. With this kind of crime, I don't care if they go away for ten years or fifty, when they come out, within months something triggers them. They're back to raping.

Let's say the victim picks someone out in the photos. Or a person comes to our attention and we show you a photo array, six photos including that person. Say, you pick out a guy, "It's number four."

What we do is work him up: check his background, where he lives, etc. We identify him as being part of an existing case.

Say, he goes after fourteen- and fifteen-year-olds in elevators. We know he's not going to stop unless we stop him.

When we find him, we arrest him. Then we contact the victim or victims and ask, "Can you come to the office for a lineup?" When you arrive, we have six people sitting in a room and you view them through a two-way mirror. There are no height markings or stuff like that. That's Los Angeles, up on the stage with the lights.

For some of you, lineups are difficult. You're reliving the event. By this point in the investigation you just want this all to go away. You won't give us an ID. We may know we have the right guy. But it's not unusual that especially a young girl, but some women, too, will say, "Oh, no, he's not there."

And we can see from the eyes that you're focused on number five. We can live with that, too. We do this so often that we can't start to let this get to us. But it does mean, without an identification, we have to let the guy go.

Dust Settles

If the guy's caught, placed under arrest, and identified, we look at the pieces of the pie that we have. There's physical evidence, information from the victim and witnesses, fingerprints, and so on. Now we want the accused's willingness to tell us the truth. To try to get that, we interview him.

When I question the accused attacker, I'm thinking about the victim. Sometimes sitting there is hard, having him go into detail about what he did to a little girl. I have to maintain a friendly voice and stay on a first-name basis.

What I'm hoping, though, is that if I gather enough information, show enough evidence against him, he will plead guilty. If he does, then the victim won't have to go to trial, go on the stand and relive the sexual assault—with the man who did it a few feet away.

My goal is to limit the exposure the victim has to the criminal justice system. It can be traumatic, and you have already endured enough trauma.

Sure, we're there with you at the various steps during the legal process. (See Chapter 17) But if I were a victim? I'd certainly feel better if I got a call that the man pleaded guilty and is going to jail, rather than getting a call saying, "You're going to have to testify."

All in all, it is a good feeling when the dust settles and we come to a case's successful conclusion.

Where Is Bruno Francisci Now? Bruno Francisci was another person who was hard to track down. With one phone number leading to another, this is what I found. After nearly a decade in the New York City Sex Crimes Squad, he transferred to the District Attorney's Office Squad. Then in 1996 after twenty-five years on the force, he retired. He now works at the Philip Morris Management Corporation.

LETTER FROM DENIKA

Janet Bode,

I read your book and just want to say thank you. Not too long ago (4 days), I was raped. Well, I think it was rape. Let me tell you my story.

My friend and I had been at the mall. Two guys we know drove up and said, "Come here." We went over to the car, talked for a while, and they asked us to sneak out with them later. We said, "OK," thinking it was harmless.

They picked us up later, after I had drunk a bottle of Cisco and a 40-ounce beer. I was plastered and they knew it. We were driving around and one of the boys started to kiss me. I didn't care, but I didn't want it to go much further. Then they went by the 7/Eleven and got condoms. The driver took us to a field and told my friend to go on a walk with him. I didn't think anything of it. At first.

The next thing I knew the other guy took off my pants, put on the condom and pulled my panties apart. I said, "You're taking advantage of me." He said, "If you say so," but he continued to do what he was doing. I wanted him to stop, but I didn't know how to say it. Remember, I was drunk. My friend came back to the car, opened the door and said, "Let's get out of here."

I said, "OK," but as soon as I stood up on both feet, I fell down on the ground. It hurt too much to walk. I hadn't been a virgin, but had had the same thing happen before about two weeks earlier by one of his friends. I woke up the next morning feeling pain inside and out.

I saw the guy last night. He just waved and smiled. I feel so used. Please tell me, was it rape? I think so!

Sincerely,

Denika

Dear Denika,

You were raped.

If you didn't want to have sex and yet you did, you were raped. If you were too drunk to be able to say "stop" clearly and the guy knew he was doing this without your permission, you were raped. Most likely the guys had a plan and did what they wanted. It didn't just happen.

Your job now is to make order from the emotional chaos that surrounds you. Where do you start? You could set aside time to do some serious thinking. Reading between the lines of your letter, I worry what else is going on in your life.

Are things a mess at home, at school, with friends, with a combination of those? As a result, do you feel overwhelmed? Depressed? Confused? Do you know why you're binge drinking? Why you're taking such chances with your life?

I realized a long time ago that life comes with problems, some horrendous, some pretty ordinary. But there are

112

solutions, too. There are ways to move beyond the past and whatever's bothering you. I talk about my problems—sometimes in a support group, as with after the rape; sometimes just with friends and family members. I write about what's troubling me, too. I go online to see what kind of help is out there, figuring I can learn from others who've experienced the same things I have. I'm also physical. I swim a few times a week, walk I don't know how many miles, and ride a bike. All that seems to help me sort out my thoughts, calm me down, and reduce the stress

I think each of us has to decide what works best in getting through and feeling good about ourselves. You have to listen to others' advice and see how it fits into the reality of your life. Try recommendations. Use the ones that feel right and discard the ones that don't. Have patience. It often takes a long time to get to the point where you are today. It often takes an equal amount of time to recover emotionally.

Finally, you should try to learn from these awful experiences—and then look to the future. Who knows, at some point down the road, you could be the one offering a steadying hand.

Thanks for writing, Denika, and I wish you well in your own journey.

Janet

CHAPTER 16

WHAT HAPPENS IN THE EMERGENCY ROOM?

If you've just been raped, even when you think you're physically all right, don't rule out seeing a doctor. To begin with, you can be tested for sexually transmitted diseases (STDs) and any pre-rape pregnancy. You can also be checked for physical damage to your body.

Another reason to do this is so medical evidence can be gathered, if you report the rape to the police. In any case, you can go to a physician, a clinic, or a hospital emergency room.

The choice is yours.

In larger cities, designated hospitals have special programs to help sexual assault survivors. One such program can be found at Brooklyn's Long Island College Hospital, where the emergency room staff, Harriet Lessel (see Chapter 10), and rape survivor advocates work together to ease your pain.

If you seek help at this kind of medical facility, the nurse who assists during the exam could be someone like Lynn Hahn, R.N., C.E.N., in the emergency department. At the age of nine, she decided she wanted to be a nurse. "I love helping people," says this down-home professional. Now it's been her job of a lifetime.

We talk during the lunch break she takes in the cramped nurses' lounge. She and the other staff come here to get off their feet for a few minutes, grab a quick snack, and change in and out of their uniforms. We start by discussing why most teenagers don't seem to want medical attention after a rape.

—— LYNN HAHN, R.N., C.E.N. ——

Afraid and Ashamed

To tell you the truth, I know that lots of teenagers don't like getting medical treatment in general. I've got four grown kids and I remember how they were. You think you don't need a doctor. You're healthy. Nothing bad can happen to you.

Then you're raped. It's such an overwhelming experience, you don't know what to do. You're afraid and ashamed. Often you don't want people to know. Plus, a hospital emergency room can be a scary place.

In this situation, though, you should see a doctor. Don't let the white uniforms upset you. Doctors and nurses are human, too. We do not judge. We're here to help you.

Nervous and Frightened

If you've been raped, you often feel dirty. You shower and douche and do all these other things. Do not, under any circumstance, douche. If there is still sperm in your body, a douche can facilitate its entry into your uterus to impregnate you. And if there's any chance you might report the attack to the police, get medical care immediately. Don't even change clothes.

At the hospital, you walk through the door and, sure, you're probably nervous and frightened. I wouldn't be surprised if it was a weekend night or the early hours of the morning. Most of the rapes we see come in at that time, especially in summer. Anyway, you say to this person we call a triage nurse, "I'm the survivor of a rape."

In our hospital—but not everywhere—that nurse takes you into a private room. We also have an advocate program here, something that doesn't happen everywhere either. As soon as we know you're a rape survivor, an advocate comes to the hospital to answer your questions and give you support.

The nurse in charge has to ask what happened and so will the doctor, the gynecologist. You have to answer questions like, "Did the perpetrator ejaculate?" "Was there oral sex?" "Anal sex?" "Was this your first time?"

We need to find these things out to know what parts of your body to check. You might have been orally raped as well as vaginally. Maybe you were knocked around. We have to know to check your mouth, to look for bruises, to talk to you about the possibility of pregnancy—and to help you through it emotionally.

During this time, I want to calm your fears to what's next: "You'll put on a hospital gown and the doctor will do a physical—check your eyes and your throat, your heart and your lungs, blood pressure, pulse, and temperature. Then you'll have a pelvic." I explain that some of the testing may be embarrassing. It's not painful, but sometimes it's uncomfortable.

I also tell you that it's in your best interest to have this exam. Why? Not just for your health and to screen for STDs and pregnancy, but if they do catch the lowlife who did it, we have the evidence to help prosecute.

You see, if you come to the hospital within, say, twenty-four hours of the rape, part of the doctor's job is to gather as much physical evidence from you as he or she can. Then that's turned over to the police.

Rape is a crime. We have to notify the police. If you walk out of this emergency room and, for example, hemorrhage to death, that becomes murder, too. But it's still your choice about reporting. You don't have to. No one—not us or the police—will force you.

Shaky and Embarrassed

Now, let's say you've never had a pelvic exam before. Under the best conditions, no one likes having one. You're in this vulnerable position—on your back on an examining table with your feet up in stirrups.

A doctor you've never seen before is going to put something into your vagina. For you, maybe it feels like another violation. This is where the advocates help the staff. By this time one has arrived at the hospital emergency room. That person asks the rape survivor, "Would you like me to stay in the room while you're being checked?"

If you like, the advocate stands by your head. She holds your hand if you want that. She's there for you. She's the shoulder to cry on, too, if you want that. And sometimes she encourages you to cry. It does help. Because some victims are crying when they come in, not everyone needs to be told that.

They're shaky. Their heads are down—which shows their embarrassment. I tell them, "You've done nothing wrong. It wasn't your fault. It's nothing for you to be ashamed of."

Then sometimes survivors are in such shock that they don't even seem fazed by the rape. But then afterwards, thinking about it, reliving it, they're hit by it. All these reactions are normal.

Ripped and Stained

Once the doctor arrives, most will tell you—the patient—what they're doing as they go along. (And, by the way, you can ask to have a woman doctor if it matters to you.) The procedure takes fifteen minutes to a half hour.

Here's what happens in the examining room if you go to the hospital soon after the rape: we have a special box called an Evidence Collection Kit.

Each one is numbered and has a checklist of what a doctor must do. If your clothes are ripped or stained, we take them for evidence, along with your panties. You might bring a change of clothing, or the hospital will provide you with something to wear home.

If there's any stuff like dirt or leaves or rug fibers on you, we put those in special evidence envelopes, too. We also comb your pubic hair to see if there's any evidence of sperm, clothing, or the other person's hair. And we comb the hair on your head.

After that, the doctor puts a speculum in your vagina and takes a smear, a specimen, to see if there's sperm present and to diagnose infection. At the same time, he or she is doing a visual check for any lacerations or discoloration of the vagina and cervix.

Next the doctor removes the speculum and inserts one or two fingers into the vagina to see if there's swelling, displacement of the ovaries, or a pregnancy.

If there was anal or oral sex, the doctor takes smears of those areas with thin Q-tips. Or maybe you say, "I scratched his face." Then we take fingernail scrapings. If you say that you were thrown down, or you're complaining of a pain in your shoulder, we might X-ray you. Other than that, we don't. When you are badly hurt and bruised, if you give us permission, photographs might be taken. Again, this is useful for police evidence.

After that, I draw blood and get a urine sample. The blood is to check for venereal disease, but not AIDS (Acquired Immune Deficiency Syndrome). With AIDS, one sexual encounter is probably not going to give it to you. If you know that the attacker is a drug abuser or bisexual, you should consider having a blood test for AIDS later.

The urine sample is to check for urinary infection or pregnancy. We call those pre-existing conditions. Ninety percent of the time we'll give you a shot, an antibiotic to prevent gonorrhea. We then give you written information about what to do for a follow-up exam six weeks later.

During that follow-up we make sure you don't have syphilis and test to see if the rapist, God forbid, got you pregnant. At some hospitals during that first exam, if you're seen within seventy-two hours of the rape, they'll give you something to prevent pregnancy. Here we don't. If you get pregnant, you can still have an abortion in most states. That's your choice.

Freed In 1992 After DNA Test, Man Is Again Convicted of Rape

HAUPPAUGE, NY., July 18 —Kerry Kotler, a convicted rapist who was freed in 1992 when DNA test results seemed to show he had been wrongly convicted, was convicted today of rape in another case . . . .

After the rape, Mr. Kotler used a water bottle to rinse his semen out of the woman's body, telling her he was washing away the evidence. . . . In 1981, before DNA testing for criminal trials was developed, Mr. Kotler was convicted of raping a woman twice in three years.

The New York Times
July 19, 1997
—AP

Even if you don't get to a doctor right after the rape, you should see one as soon as possible. A month later, two months

119

later, you can still be checked for infections, pregnancy, and peace of mind. Whenever you come, just remember that you'll get all the support the nurses and doctors can give you.

Where Is Lynn Hahn Now? Lynn Hahn has become a grandmother, lost her dear husband, and been promoted. She is now the Nurse Manager of the Emergency Department of Long Island College Hospital.

While the medical procedures for rape survivors have remained generally the same, we have more information about HIV and AIDS. Recent findings show that 99 percent of people infected with HIV seroconvert—go from negative to positive—within thirty days of possible infection.

This means that survivors could know a month after a rape, shortening the time they have to worry about whether they contracted the virus. Also, other studies are beginning to reveal that if treated immediately with a "cocktail" of drugs, HIV may be stopped before it begins.

When asked why she thinks more rapists seem to be putting on condoms before a sexual assault, Hahn says fear of AIDS is her best guess.

CHAPTER 17

THE ACCUSED'S RIGHTS ARE GREATER THAN THE VICTIM'S

To find out what happens once lawyers and judges get involved in a rape case, I question three people: a defense attorney, Barry Slotnick; a prosecuting attorney, Linda Fairstein; and a noted judge, who asks not to be quoted by name.

Slotnick, opinionated and brilliant, often defends people whose names and deeds make news. He's represented Mafia bosses, clergy, and a Long Island (New York) teenager accused of murdering his ex-girlfriend during "rough" sex.

Linda Fairstein, a hands-on activist lawyer, has been the Chief of the Sex Crimes Prosecution Unit of New York County's District Attorney's Office for more than two decades. Despite her heavy administrative workload, she feels she must still periodically try some cases herself. Her professional colleagues describe her as driven, yet fair.

During separate interviews, Slotnick, Fairstein, and the judge are asked to explain a "typical" rape case from their own legal perspective. We start with a definition of the crime, then go step by step through the complex legal process.

1. The crime is committed.

FAIRSTEIN: Each state in the country has a slightly different definition of rape. The general concept, though, is that it's sexual intercourse without the consent of the victim. There has to be penetration of the penis into the vagina, however slight, but ejaculation isn't necessary.

To sustain a charge of *first* degree rape, there has to be some force, too. This can be physical force, the use of a weapon, or a verbal threat: "Do what I tell you or I'll hurt you." (With statutory rape, rape of a minor, no force is needed.)

In all states, it's also against the law and just as serious when there is forced contact between the defendant's penis and the victim's mouth, between the defendant's penis and the victim's anus, or between the defendant's mouth and the victim's vagina.

2. A man is arrested and charged.

JUDGE: In any crime, rape included, the accused is guaranteed certain rights. These stem from the underlying principal in our justice system—a person is presumed innocent until proven guilty. From that flow additional rights.

For example, the accused has an absolute right to counsel, a lawyer. If he doesn't have a lawyer or can't afford one, one will be assigned. The accused's rights are greater than those of the victim and the reason for that is fairness. When you have the potential to deprive someone of liberty to walk the streets as a free person, it must be done in a legally proper manner.

SLOTNICK: Maybe you think it's reprehensible for a lawyer to represent someone who's been accused of rape. But where do you draw the line? What happens if teachers or students or

Republicans become unpopular? Is it then reprehensible for a lawyer to represent them?

I do have problems with people accused of child molesting. If I believe they're guilty, I won't represent them. I feel that subconsciously I wouldn't do the most effective job.

Other than that, would I represent somebody if I knew he had done it? Sure. The system has nothing to do with guilt or innocence. It has to do with what's proven or not proven. And the burden of proof is on the accuser to prove beyond a reasonable doubt that the other person, my client, committed the crime.

Say Jack the Ripper comes into my office. I find out a bit about the crime. I feel I can represent him effectively. He has the ability to properly compensate me—pay my bill. I agree to take the case.

Now one thing I won't do is put him on the witness stand to lie. But it's the prosecutor's job to prove the case. That's who's making the accusation.

Well, with Jack the Ripper, everybody's sure he's the one, and the prosecutor decides to try the case based on that speculation. Now let's say he gets convicted. The media has predisposed the jury to believe this is Jack the Ripper, yet the prosecutor does not demonstrate that he is.

Justice hasn't been done, even though he's guilty. When you convict one person on less than good evidence—even though he's guilty—the danger is the next person may also be convicted on less than good evidence, and he's innocent.

3. The rape survivor has a series of interviews with a member of the prosecutor's legal office to see what proof there is that a crime has been committed

FAIRSTEIN: A rape victim needs more care, more compassion, more of a relationship with the person prosecuting the case. You also need to be directed to the other resources, such as counseling. So the first time we meet you, we explain the system.

My role as a prosecutor is to do justice. I represent the state. Technically, I'm not the victim's lawyer. The victim is a witness like any other witness, but certainly the main witness, the complaining witness. If I take the case to trial, that means I believe completely in you—the victim.

We try to gain your trust and confidence to get the facts that we need to proceed. Yes, we need to know everything that happened. To do that we need to ask very personal questions. One element that victims often leave out is drug and/or alcohol involvement.

We had a case where an upper-middle-class teenager told us she was taken at knifepoint by a street bum into a store to buy sodas, onto a subway, past policemen, and finally to a secluded area where he raped her. That didn't make sense.

I told her what I believed and what I didn't believe. After working with her for an hour, she admitted what really took place. She'd met this guy who'd offered her an ounce of marijuana and fifty dollars if she would come with him to where he kept his stash to help roll joints to sell. For the adventure, whatever, she agreed. Once there, he pulled the knife.

Another element a victim sometimes covers up is some part of a relationship with the accused, especially when he's an acquaintance. If, for example, you've been going to the home of the accused after school and making out with him, but not wanting to have sex, I've got to know that. (And I won't tell your parents all the details.)

If you've been sending him love letters for the last six weeks and now regret it, that doesn't mean you were going to sleep with him. Still I've got to know about the letters. The guy—the defendant—can walk into court, produce them, and there goes the case.

CRY RAPE

> **SLOTNICK:** There are a lot of people who cry rape who are not forcibly subjected to anything.
>
> **FAIRSTEIN:** Only occasionally do women make up allegations of rape. The stories that stay in people's minds, though, are these false reports. When we are able to interview the victim apart from other people and review the facts of the case, we're usually successful in getting her to tell us that the story of forced intercourse isn't true. We resolve the case by marking it "unfounded," which means because we have disproved certain elements, we will not take it to trial. We also get the victim appropriate counseling.

4. As the case moves through the criminal justice system, a series of legal steps is taken that varies somewhat from state to state.

JUDGE: Once the accused is arrested, that person is brought before a judge at the earliest possible point. The prosecuting attorney, a person such as Fairstein, tells the judge the facts of the case. Based on that information, the judge makes an independent decision as to the appropriate bail.

The victim doesn't have to be present.

Some states have a second hearing, a preliminary or pretrial hearing. In other states, the case is sent directly to a grand jury where the jurors decide whether to indict.

During this time, what is called plea bargaining occurs. The defense lawyer for the accused sits down with the prosecutor to talk about the case. Maybe he says, "My client will enter a guilty plea in exchange for having the complaint lowered to something less serious."

The prosecutor says, "Okay." Or maybe the prosecutor says, "No, the man's a repeat offender with loads of evidence against him."

If they can't agree, the case goes to trial.

There is usually a delay of six more months to a year before I hear the case in my courtroom. This happens for two reasons: (1) our criminal justice system is overburdened and (2) often the defense strategy is to delay as long as possible.

The Constitution entitles the accused to a speedy and fair trial. However, in reality, he hopes that as time passes, the accuser—you, the rape victim—will disappear, change your mind about testifying, or simply forget certain details. The advantage of a faded memory is if you testify differently at trial from the way you've previously testified, say, at a preliminary hearing, then the defense lawyer can confront you with your inconsistent statements.

He can say, "Ladies and gentlemen of the jury, first she testified that the man who raped her had blue eyes. Now she says he had brown eyes. She is not believable." And therefore the accused, his client, should be found not guilty.

The accused also has an absolute right to a face-to-face confrontation with the accuser. In any criminal case, the accuser—here that means the rape victim—has to appear in court, tell the story, and be subjected to cross-examination by a lawyer for the accused.

5. The lawyers prepare for the trial.

SLOTNICK: It's difficult to analyze a rape case. You're dealing with emotional perceptions. With a bank robbery, you walk into a bank, stick a gun in somebody's face, say, "Give me the money," and leave.

Sexual assault is not always so black and white. Sexual

assault to one person may be a beckoning to another. Especially when two people know each other, the accused may say, "I didn't do anything that she didn't want me to do."

And in his mind, he honestly believes that there was consent to what the woman is now saying was sexual assault. For the woman, what was fine on Tuesday, the recollection turns into rape by Friday.

What I look for in a case, though, is how long ago it took place, where, and the circumstances. Did they know each other beforehand to the point that they were sexually involved? During the alleged incident was there a physical struggle? Was someone immediately told about it? What was the state of mind of the complainant, the accuser? Does she run around saying that everybody is assaulting her?

I look at all those elements—and then hope my client was in Acapulco at the time of the incident.

FAIRSTEIN: Rape cases between strangers are generally easier to prosecute. Unlike any other kind of crime, sexual assaults are contact crimes that take a lot of time to happen. A short sex offense has the victim with the offender for fifteen minutes and often for hours.

So what we try to do when we investigate is say to the victim, "Let's take that time and use it against the guy. The reason I'm pressing you to think about everything that was said and done is this.

"You saw this man with all your senses working. There was a tremendous amount of contact. We've got to retrieve that information to build as strong a case as possible."

Rape between acquaintances has been and continues to be difficult. By difficult, I don't mean my job, but for the victim. There is usually an attempt by the defense attorney to blame the victim for participation.

Soft Spot for Serial Murder

According to a Senate Judiciary Committee study on violence against women, rape rose faster than any other reported violent crime in America. Though 100,000 rapes are reported every year, the report estimates that the actual number is really between 1.3 and 2 million. Our rape rate is the world's highest.

We tolerate a staggering rate of sexual assault on our daughters. Some social psychologists think that as many as 40 percent of our little girls are assaulted by their fathers or other men in their lives. No one puts the number at less than 25 percent. . . ."

The New York Times
April 28, 1991
—by Sara Paretski

Because it is someone you know, it's often somebody you trusted. You think, "He's okay. I go to school with him. I can't believe he did that." And these cases are overwhelmingly the ones with delayed reporting. Often the victim has failed to take advantage of what medical evidence there might be, making the case even harder to prove.

Part of the trial preparation is trying to make the victim comfortable in knowing what to expect in the courtroom. We review the facts and the story with you and explain the cross-examination procedure. We tell you what the defense lawyer is allowed to ask, what questions I will object to that you then won't have to answer, and the truth that there are some things we don't know. We don't know if there are some questions a judge will make you answer.

6. The trial generally lasts a few days, but on occasion runs longer. The survivor, the accused, the lawyers, judge, jury, witnesses, and interested spectators are allowed in the courtroom.

JUDGE: I tell juries that a trial proceeds in the conventional way they've read about in books or seen on TV—except we're not as sleazy as *L.A. Law*. I expect a lawyer to stand up when addressing me or the jury.

With a rape trial, all sorts of thoughts go through my mind. When anyone is testifying, because I'm the judge, I've got to exercise complete control over my facial expressions. My internal emotions, though, can range from extreme sympathy to extreme rage.

In a date rape or a rape by a family member, the victim could well be asked about the nature of prior contact with the person. The emphasis would be on whether you consented and whether there's a motive to lie.

If it's a stranger, then the questioning goes more to the issue of mistaken identification. While the judge can't protect you against aggressive cross-examination, you have to trust that the court system operates on good faith. We don't want to hurt people.

I feel that rape is an antiwoman crime. It's not so much a sexual crime as a crime of terrible viciousness. It should always be reported if the person can deal with it. By reporting, you are setting the wheels in motion not only to punish the attacker for this act, but in all likelihood to prevent him from doing it to someone else.

SLOTNICK: All parts of a trial are important, and it's all about participation. It's not a spectator sport. The prosecutor and I select the jury. I partake. I speak to the jury. I wave my hands. I raise my voice. I present my witnesses, nice people who know the defendant and can attest to his fine character.

I cross-examine the prosecutor's witnesses. I try to do damage to their testimony.

When the accuser is on the stand, I'm thinking, "Is what she's saying possible? Where are the inconsistencies in what she's saying today and what she said in the past? What does she say occurred first? Can she prove it?

"She says the man took her to a motel? Is there a registration form that he signed? Why didn't she report it right away? She didn't tell her best friend? She didn't tell her sister? Hmm."

And then, of course, "What's her motive in all this?" It wasn't rape; it was fun. It was fun until the authorities and the adults got into the picture. You know adults.

I've got to make a tactical decision. When I come on like an ogre it may stimulate the witness to show a side that the jury hasn't seen. At the same time, I don't want my attack to antagonize the jury and engender sympathy for the witness.

Then during this whole process, I am building the foundation for my final argument to the jury. I hope to convince them that my client should be found not guilty.

It's a little like being an actor, but I don't have a script. And if I do it wrong the first time, I can't do it over again.

Waiting for the verdict is the most difficult part.

I can't make small talk. I can't read. All I can do is pace.

Then when it's over, I feel strange.

The good Lord has been kind to me. I've won most of my cases. Most of my clients walk out with the jury saying, "Not guilty, not guilty, not guilty." Everybody hugs and kisses. They're happy. Maybe I go out to dinner with my wife. The following morning, I don't have to go to court and it's lonely. I'm very down—until the next case.

FAIRSTEIN: A lot of teenagers have questions about who can and cannot be in the courtroom. If you—the victim—want a parent, your whole family, a support team there, that's fine. However, some people worry about the parents' reactions and don't want them to hear exactly what happened, for whatever reasons. In those cases, we ask the parents to stay in the waiting area next door.

Even though the defendant has a constitutional right to be present, there are ways for you to get through the trial without looking at him or only looking at him when you have to identify him. You can look at us, the jury, or your support people.

Yes, it is difficult—even harrowing—to relate the story in the presence of the man you're accusing. But this is your chance to see justice done. If you're uncomfortable for two hours, four hours, or however long you have to testify, look beyond to the goal you're accomplishing. Without testifying, he would walk free without appropriate sanctions.

Aside from the victim, we call witnesses, such as the first person to whom you made an outcry. Often that's a friend who saw you and said, "Don't keep this to yourself." This person can testify, "She'd been crying. Her blouse was torn."

Sometimes in an acquaintance rape, the victim might have been at a party with ten other people and left with one of them. A person might testify, "When they left together they were not holding hands. She had not been drinking."

A medical person who treated the victim might be called as a witness, as would police investigators who have anything to contribute.

The defendant is allowed to testify, as well, although he usually chooses not to. If the defendant does take the stand, we would then cross-examine him. We also cross-examine any of his witnesses.

From my perspective, we prepare the victim for the problems with the case. But we can't promise the outcome. It's decided by a jury of twelve people.

While waiting for the verdict, my usual advice is to go home, do something else, and tell me where I can reach you. Then if you want to be around when the jury reads the verdict, we keep you company. In my years with the Sex Crimes Prosecution Unit, our conviction rate has never been lower than 75 percent a year, and it has been as high as 90 percent.

7. If the defendant is found guilty, about a month or so later, he is sentenced by the same judge who heard the case.

JUDGE: Before sentencing, I get a probation report. It gives me the person's background: family, education, and any previous criminal record. Usually there's been an interview with the probation officer, the prosecuting attorney, and maybe with the victim.

I try not to make my final decision until after reading the report, as well as hearing one last time from the prosecutor, the defendant's lawyer, and the defendant. Then with all that and a certain gut reaction, I announce the sentence.

NOTE: A rape survivor can also bring a civil suit against the rapist and/or against what's known as a third party; for example, the landlord of the building where the rape occurred. To learn more about this procedure, ask a rape crisis center advocate or a lawyer.

Where Are They Now? The judge wishes to remain anonymous. Barry Slotnick continues to represent a wide range of famous and infamous people in his New York City law practice. In addition to her normal workload, Linda Fairstein has

New Jersey, Megan's Home, Limits "Her" Law

Months ago, Alaska posted a list of its 1,600 paroled sex offenders on the World Wide Web. California provides information on about 64,000 offenders on CD-ROM at any county sheriff's office or big-city police department. And three months ago, Connecticut began letting local police stations release the names, addresses, and pictures of paroled offenders to anyone who calls

But in New Jersey, the state that inspired the nationwide movement for public warnings about the presence of sex offenders, information is held far more tightly

The New York Times
January 5, 7998
—by Robert Hanley

become a writer of nonfiction and fiction. Her first book was published in 1993 and is titled *Sexual Violence: Our War Against Rape*. She is now writing a series of well-reviewed mysteries. The first two are *Final Jeopardy* and *Likely to Die*, both published by Scribners.

Prevention

CHAPTER 18

YOUR POWER TO END RAPE

Each person I interview, I ask, "How do we prevent rape?" Some of them hesitate. "We don't use the word 'prevent,'" says the rape crisis center advocate. "That puts the responsibility on the person raped. You're saying the person could have done something to stop the rapist—prevent the crime. That isn't the case."

However, those I talk to do agree: changing laws won't stop rape, only changing people will. Where you have to begin, they suggest, is by examining your own life, attitudes, and behavior. This means you may have to make serious life changes, a step many adults can't or won't take. As teenagers, though, you are more capable of change. Your beliefs aren't yet set in such hard concrete. It is in your power to end rape.

Below are specific steps you can take that will make male readers less likely to rape and female readers less likely to be victims. At a minimum, experts who have studied the circumstances of sexual assaults and their outcomes say that those women and girls who mentally prepare for the possibility and rehearse responses are best able to keep a completed rape from happenng.

Break the Cycle

Have you been or are you being physically or sexually abused? Physical or sexual violence is *not* a way to communicate. It can lead to lifelong problems from uncontrollable anger to inability to form loving relationships.

Just as true, for every action, there is a reaction. The young victims of today often grow up to become the adult offenders of tomorrow.

Do everything in your power to break the cycle. Go public. Get as many people as you can involved in helping you change that dangerous situation. It may be difficult to let people know what's happening, but it won't be more emotionally painful than what you're going through.

If you need to remain anonymous for a while, first contact a crisis center or hotline. Tell them and ask for advice. Then tell a friend, and tell another. Better yet, **tell a wise adult you trust what is happening.** (Now look ahead to page 143 for further advice offered to female survivors that could benefit you, too.)

Have you already flashed, spied, sexually abused, or sexually assaulted others? If the answer is yes, again, tell a trusted adult before you become more of a danger to yourself and to others.

Robbing a person of material possessions is a crime. Stealing a person's emotional security is worse. Don't take what isn't yours.

Read Chapters 4, 6, and 9, the rape survivors' stories, as well as the letters. Listen to the experiences of others who have been sexually assaulted or abused. If you are guilty of this behavior, think about the consequences of your actions. Think about your destructive effect on others.

Stop giving yourself permission to cause such pain. It is not too late to ask forgiveness. In person, over the phone or in writing, apologize to those you've hurt.

Mixed Messages

You want to fool around, but your date says no? No means no. It doesn't mean maybe. It doesn't mean "no" now, but "yes" in a few minutes. If you have to force, scare, or threaten her before she goes along with what you want sexually, that's rape.

Against her will is against the law.

You think the girl you're with is sending you a mixed message about sex? Ask her. That's right. Stop and say to her, "What do you want?" If she can't tell you, don't have sex with her. She's playing a game with you. You want shared responsibility for sexual decisions.

You feel inadequate? Insecure? You have periods of anger and frustration? How you relieve these emotions should never include taking them out on another person.

You talk a lot about who's gotten laid and who hasn't, which girls are easy and which aren't, and what are your next sexual plans with whom? You use violent language when referring to females?

Think about your conversations. If your words treat females as objects instead of human beings you respect, you're revealing an attitude that allows rape to happen.

Many rapes begin in party situations. Friends encourage friends to go along with the game of the moment. Rat packs of jocks in particular have been known to turn partying into rape-as-a-contact-sport.

In groups, you're less likely to look into your heart about what's right and what's wrong, and more likely to just go along for the ride.

In groups, you think that even if you're caught, there'll be less blame. This is not true. **Resist peer pressure.** Be the one who helps the potential victim, not the next to jump on the train.

Don't convince yourself that a drunk or drugged female is fair game. Don't think that if she has no memory of what happened, you're home safe. That's dead wrong. What's right is that drinking and drugging reduce your own ability, too. They bring out a kind of aggressive arrogance. You're less able to take care of yourself and control the situation you're in.

⎯⎯ GIRLS/WOMEN ⎯⎯

Set Limits

Don't put control of your life in someone else's hands. Right now, think about what you want from a date, how far you want to go sexually, and if you even want sex in the relationship.

It's up to you—not a date—to make decisions about your life, your body, and your sexual self. Then set limits. Be absolutely clear and consistent with words and actions: "I will go this far, but no further."

When you're a teenager, you're learning about life. That's your job. Many of you, though, put yourselves in risky situations. **Have a back-up plan.** When you're out, let someone know where you are. If you're out late, have a safe way home. Take at least enough money for a phone call, or better yet, transportation.

If you're on a first date with a boy you don't know well, stick to public places—a movie, a mall, a restaurant. **Use common sense.** Don't let him convince you you'll have more fun at some deserted park, an empty beach, or his home with no one else there.

Dump 'Em

Pick your dates with care.

- Dump them if they hit, slap, or push you around.
- Dump them if they're overly possessive, jealous, and controlling.
- Dump them if they always want things done their way.
- Dump them if they always put you down.
- Dump them if they don't back off when you say stop.
- Dump them if even your best girlfriend warns you about their bad reputations.

These guys are more likely to rape.

When you're with people you don't know well, **trust your instincts.** If you feel uncomfortable even if you can't quite figure out why, leave. So what if they call you a geek. It's better to feel uncool than to be attacked.

If a boy you've just met says, "Here's some ecstasy," some pot, whatever, be on guard. Some rapists figure you won't report them if you've done something illegal, too. Drinking and drugging reduce your ability to take care of yourself and control the situation you're in.

What If?

Plan ahead. Think to yourself, "What would I do if someone assaulted me?" Picture yourself in different situations. What if someone broke into your house, approached you outdoors, or trapped you in a car? How could you get away without hurting yourself? What are your strengths? Your weaknesses? Can you run fast? Really scream? Do you know parts of the body that feel the most pain—like shins, eyes, the bridge of the nose, the Adam's apple, the groin.

What natural weapons do you have? Maybe you carry keys, or hair spray. Put the keys between your fingers and use them to scratch the guy. Aim at the eyes with the hair spray or if the can's big enough, hit him with it.

Remember though, any weapon is only as good as the person who uses it. It can also be taken away and used against you. If you feel safer carrying something for protection, make sure you can get to it quickly. When it's buried at the bottom of your day pack, it's useless.

Strangers who rape count on an easy target and startling their victim. This is how they have the advantage. Do something to surprise them to try to throw them off balance: pretend to faint, act crazy, or vomit on the assailant.

Learn basic self-defense strategies, from how to make a fist (thumb outside) to how to attract attention. Unless you know what you're doing, don't try to be Wonder Woman and fight an armed assailant. You only want to catch him off-guard to give you a chance to get away as fast as possible.

Safety-Check

Be suspicious of strangers. Say, you're waiting for an elevator and you don't like the way this other person is looking at you. Don't get in. If the person hassles you, make a scene or run away.

Especially in stranger rape situations, try to make yourself *real* to the attacker. For instance, say to him, "I don't know you. I've never done anything to you. Why are you doing this to me?" Try to break through what this man says to himself to justify rape.

Many rapes happen in homes and apartments. When you're alone, it's safer not to open the door until you know who it is. If it's a repair person, ask for identification. If you still feel uncomfortable, call where the person works and find out whether anyone was sent to your home.

Don't be embarrassed to keep a person waiting or not let him in at all.

Check the safety where you live. Rapes sometimes occur because of inadequate security. For example, entrances should be well lighted and windows should be undamaged, with locks. If you live in the basement or first-floor apartment, bars could be installed.

It's smart to have curtains for protection and privacy. Doors that lead outside should have strong locks. You should pay special attention to places where a possible assailant might hide—under stairwells, between buildings, and in areas protected by trees, shrubs, or bushes.

If you think improvements are needed, talk to a parent. Renters, go to the owner and ask for repairs to protect everyone from unwanted intruders.

Street Smart

To try to safety-proof your life on the street. Be aware of what's happening around you, especially at night or when you're in places you don't know well. **Walk with a don't-mess-with-me attitude.** That's often enough to convince strangers to look for an easier target.

After dark, try to avoid unlighted parking lots, alleys, and shortcuts through deserted areas. Even on lighted streets, if you hear voices or footsteps behind you, check them out. If you think someone might be following you, change your pace to slower or faster. If that doesn't work, cross the street or even walk down the middle of the road. **If you're still worried, start screaming "fire." You'll get help more quickly than if you yell "rape."**

Reveal the Secret

If you've been molested or raped by some known or unknown person, ignoring its impact won't make the emotional crisis decrease. If you can't talk about it today, at least start a journal. Write down your thoughts about this experience and how it colors your life at this moment.

Then with time, gather your courage and turn to others to help diffuse the pain. Tell all the trusted people in your life what has occurred. Ask them for their ongoing support to aid you in reclaiming your life. Tell them you don't want to turn your own sense of outrage and worthlessness into inappropriate actions with others. Will they be there for you?

If you are currently being abused, there is more urgency to go public. Reveal the secret. By doing that, you might be surprised to learn how many others have gone through a similar trauma. Many violators don't molest one person once and stop. They don't rape once and stop.

Their actions follow a pattern distinct to each of them, and with time the level of emotional and physical violence they create may escalate. They may commit increasingly more serious offenses. They may tire of you and go after an even younger victim.

This, too, cannot be denied. A charge of incest can rip through a family like a tornado. Afterwards everything is different. Social workers, children's services personnel, school officials, the courts, the police—all may get involved. There is always the chance people will doubt you are telling the truth. That disbelief is just another form of abuse. Don't give up hope. All children—yourself included—are resilient. You can have a better life for having told.

And now, go back to page 137 and read the short section aimed at boys and men on breaking the cycle. What applies to them could have meaning for you.

Program stops generational pattern of childhood abuse, teen pregnancy

. . . the childhood experience of sexual abuse has profound, long-term influences on the thinking and behavior of victims. . . .

An abusive childhood can mean an adult who is not sufficiently prepared to respond to the stresses of the world or, heartbreakingly, to the stresses of parenting. . . . All research indicates substantial numbers of people are abused as children: about 12 percent of men and 17 percent of women were sexually touched by adults before reaching the age of 13 years.

There seems to be a link between the experiencing of childhood sexual abuse and childbearing in adolescence. A majority of adolescent mothers in two surveys reported that they had been sexually abused as children. . . .

The Brown University Child and
Adolescent Behavior Letter
August 1997
—by Harriet Meyer

—— BOYS AND GIRLS/MEN AND WOMEN ——

In most school systems, if an adult suspects a student has been physically abused, a reporting procedure exists. Determining sexual abuse is more difficult. The wounds are internal. But again, there are steps to follow. This often isn't true when it comes to the issues of dating violence, date rape, or rape by a stranger.

Stopping Rape

- Get to know the minds and hearts of the opposite sex.
- Hang out together.
- Learn to be friends, to trust each other, before you ever consider becoming lovers.
- Male or female, don't be afraid to be seen as the person who stands up for what is right.
- Do whatever it takes—from sports to therapy to prayer—in order to feel strong and positive about yourself.
- Find one thing to really care about. Then put as much energy into being good at that as you ever would into being bad or tearing yourself down.

Ask a teacher or counselor whether there is a school procedure to follow. If there is no plan, work together to develop one. Ask that, at a minimum, each student participate in a serious discussion of what is rape, why does it happen, and what can be done to reduce the incidence of this crime.

The Law

The rape laws are changing. Since 1993, not only date rape, but also marital rape is a crime in all fifty states. Unless you have flat-out permission to touch another person sexually, according to the law, it can be judged rape.

The language is clear. You need positive, explicit consent. It must be freely, voluntarily, and intelligently given. That consent cannot be impaired by alcohol and other drugs.

Put simply: You can't take anything without asking and receiving permission.

It's about honoring each other's boundaries, being sensitive to each other's needs. It's about mutual respect. It's about stopping rape.

Your Goal

I'd like to be able to recommend you report all cases of sexual abuse and assault. If police stations are flooded with reports, maybe then people would recognize the dimension of this violence—a violence that is more often directed against women. Maybe then, people would work together to end this crime.

Right now, many attackers don't think there are consequences for their actions.

Let them know times are changing. Let them experience that sense of powerlessness when they are picked up by the police on rape charges. No one really wants to be known as a rapist.

When Your Parents Were Teenagers

- *Few* schools had assemblies or programs to discuss the issue of sexual assault.
- *Few* mental health specialists were studying the aftershocks of rape.
- *Few* rape crisis centers existed.
- *Few* hospitals had special procedures to help rape survivors.
- *Few* police officers were required to take sensitivity training before assignment to a sex crimes unit.
- *Few* prosecuting attorneys were part of a special sex crimes prosecution unit. The wall of silence was nearly complete.

Since your parents' generation, there have been changes, just not enough. The criminal justice system has an unchanged history of not believing the word of rape survivors in general, and the younger the survivor the less likely it is that you will be believed. Before reporting, keep that in mind. Ask those you care for and trust to help you make this choice. Finally, though, you decide.

Today make it your goal to break through what remains of the silence about sexual abuse and assault. Choose to be the generation that deals directly and honestly with the issue, the generation that does more than make things a little easier for survivors who decide to go public and report.

Take the next step and say, "We will work to change attitudes and change behavior, so our children will not have to live with this outrage. We will create a society where sexual assault has ceased to exist."

Write about Rape

If you find this book helpful, look for others I've written on related topics. If you feel you can't talk to anyone about the issue of rape, putting your thoughts in writing can be beneficial. If you'd like to send me a copy, here's my address:

Janet Bode: c/o Franklin Watts/Grolier
PO Box 1333
Danbury, CT 06813-1333

To Media Specialists and Other Interested Adults

Too Many Lives

One summer day, in between editing interviews and conducting new ones, I spent the morning with a room full of women, all graduate students, all young adult media specialists in training. As with my teen audiences, I asked for their help with my work-in-progress. Would they take a few minutes to write on how rape might have touched their lives?

Their responses were revealing.

Seven knew of rape "only through the media." Of the remaining nine, two were survivors. The others wrote of the rape of a "beautiful best friend," a "sister," "a young neighborhood mother on a quiet afternoon on the tree-lined street."

I am not so direct with adolescents. Instead, I'm more likely to have them comment on what's best or worst in their lives. Their scraps of paper serve as my window into their concerns and special feelings.

Today, I'm no longer caught unaware by the number who, unprompted, mention experiencing some form of sexual assault: "A 10th-grader sexually molested me when I was in 6th grade," writes one. "The foulest thing in my life is dealing with the aftermath of date rape by a guy I trusted," writes another. "The best thing in my life is realizing that being sexually molested was not my fault," writes a third.

Rape touches too many lives—yours, mine, and our children's. From my vantage point, I've come to believe that while the teen years have always proved to be a tricky terrain, our daughters are growing up in a more dangerous environment than we did. It's meaner, and more sexual.

Just walking from class to class can be hazardous. In my files I have a clip of a nationwide survey of high-school and middle-school students. Two-thirds of the girls report being touched, grabbed, or pinched on school grounds. For one in four, the first experience of sexual intercourse occurs through rape. As I write this, the nightly news has a segment about a recent discovery that child abuse—sexual, physical, and emotional—literally causes parts of the brain to shrivel.

Over the years, librarians have told me that this book is painful to read. How well I understand; it was painful to write. I look forward to the time when it is no longer needed.

Returned and Stolen

Media specialists have also told me that *Voices of Rape* is among the most stolen books in their library collections. If students are working on a research paper, say, for a life skills or health class, usually it's checked out and returned. If the problem is personal, sometimes the best they can do is sneak it from the library. Going public remains too upsetting.

I keep both these student needs in mind when creating any project, this one included. I learn, too, from my competition— how TV, the net, the Web, documentaries, magazines, and newspapers present information.

During library visits, I watch my audience pick up my books, flip through the pages, and stop and start reading. For many the cartoon strips are the path by which they enter. Others go for the boxed information. Still others tell me they move straight through from start to finish, the real-life stories carrying them along. In this revised edition, I have shared a few letters from past readers. For them, as for me, writing combined with reading helps bring about healing.

One Kid at a Time

I thank you for placing this book on your shelves. Some of you go further. You put it directly in students' hands. You include it in a special bin where books on controversial and troubling topics are borrowed anonymously on an honor system. You add it to a section marked "Good Books" and "More Good Books," in response to the request, "Do you have any good books to read?"

I don't know if you hear about the ripple effect, the lives you guide with those gestures. "Once I hinted at my problems, my librarian showed me your book," writes yet another teenager. "Then when my boyfriend got mad because I wouldn't make love to him, I handed it to him and said, 'read this.' Afterwards he said he understood, and apologized. . . ."

When I finish letters such as that one, I have to smile. It's my reward. Helping others, changing minds on this issue, educating the future generation one kid at a time is, in my opinion, worth the pain. May you and I continue together in this effort.

Related Books

Bode, Janet. *Different Worlds: Interracial and Cross-Cultural Dating.* New York: Franklin Watts, 1989.

———. *New Kids on the Block: Oral Histories of Immigrant Teens.* New York: Franklin Watts, 1989. *New Kids in Town.* New York: Scholastic, 1991.

———. *Truce: Ending the Sibling War.* New York: Franklin Watts, 1991. *Truce: Ending the Sibling War,* New York: Dell, 1993.

——— and comic strip by Stan Mack. *Beating the Odds: Stories of Unexpected Achievers.* New York: Franklin Watts, 1991.

——— and comic strip by Stan Mack. *Kids Still Having Kids: People Talk about Teen Pregnancy.* New York: Franklin Watts, 1992.

——— and comic strips by Stan Mack. *Death Is Hard to Live With: Teenagers Talk about How They Cope with Loss.* New York: Delacorte, 1993. *Death Is Hard to Live With.* New York: Laurel-Leaf Books, 1995.

——— and comic strips by Stan Mack. *Heartbreak and Roses: Real Life Stories of Troubled Love.* New York: Delacorte, 1994. *Heartbreak and Roses.* New York: Laurel-Leaf, 1996.

———. *Trust and Betrayal: Real Life Stories of Friends and*

Enemies. New York: Delacorte, 1995. *Trust and Betrayal*. New York: Laurel-Leaf, 1997.

―― and Stan Mack. *Hard Time: A Real Life Look at Juvenile Crime and Violence*. New York: Delacorte, 1996. *Hard Time*. New York: Laurel-Leaf, 1998.

――. *Food Fight: A Guide to Eating Disorders for Pre-Teens and Their Parents*. New York: Simon & Schuster, 1997.

Boumil, Marcia M., Joel Friedman, and Barbara Ewert Taylor. *Date Rape, The Secret Epidemic: What It Is, What It Isn't, What It Does to You, What You Can Do about It*. Deerfield Beach, FL: Health Communications, 1993.

Carosella, Cynthia, editor. *Who's Afraid of the Dark? A Forum of Truth, Support, and Assurance for Those Affect by Rape*. New York: HarperPerennial, 1995.

Crowell, Nancy A., and Ann W. Burgess, editors. *Understanding Violence against Women*. Washington D.C.: National Academy Press, 1996.

Fairstein, Linda A. *Sexual Violence: Our War Against Rape*. New York: William Morrow, 1993.

Fein, Judith. *How to Fight Back and Win: The Joy of Self-Defense*. Sebastopol, CA: Torrance Publishing, 1996.

Gilmartin, Pat. *Rape, Incest, and Child Sexual Abuse: Consequences and Recovery*. New York: Garland Publishing, 1994.

Haskins, James. *The Scottsboro Boys*. New York: Henry Holt, 1994.

Hirsh, Karen D., editor. *Mind Riot: Coming of Age in Comix*. New York: Aladdin, 1997.

Johnson, Scott A. *When "I Love You" Turns Violent: Abuse in Dating Relationships*. Far Hills, NJ: New Horizon Press, 1993.

LaValle, John J. *Everything You Need to Know When You*

Are the Male Survivor of Rape or Sexual Assault. New York: Rosen Publishing Group, 1996.

Ledray, Linda. *Recovering from Rape.* 2nd edition, New York: Henry Holt, 1994.

Lefkowitz, Bernard. *Our Guys: The Glen Ridge Rape and the Secret Life of the Perfect Suburb.* Berkeley, CA: University of California Press, 1997.

Miller, Maryann. *Drugs and Date Rape.* New York: Rosen Publishing Group, 1995.

Mufson, Susan, and Sarah Kranz. *Straight Talk about Date Rape.* New York: Facts on File, 1993.

Parrot, Andrea. *Coping with Date Rape and Acquaintance Rape.* New York: Rosen Publishing Group, 1993.

Prendergast, William E. *The Merry-Go-Round of Sexual Abuse: Identifying and Treating Survivors.* Binghamton, NY: Haworth Press, 1993.

———. *Sexual Abuse of Children and Adolescents: A Preventive Guide for Parents, Teachers, and Counselors.* New York: The Continuum Publishing Company, 1996.

Roiphe, Kate. *The Morning After: Sex, Fear, and Feminism on Campus.* Boston: Little, Brown & Co., 1993.

Swisher, Karen L., and Carol Wekesser, editors, William Barbour, assistant editor. *Violence against Women.* San Diego: Greenhaven Press, 1996.

Taylor, Lawrence. *To Honor and Obey.* New York: William Morrow, 1992.

Warshaw, Robin, and Afterword by Mary P. Koss. *I Never Called It Rape: The Ms. Report on Recognizing, Fighting, and Surviving Date and Acquaintance Rape.* New York: HarperPerennial, 1994.

With Thanks

I thank my support team for always being there when I need them. Special praise goes to:

My sisters, Barbara and Carolyn; and my extended family, Pearl, Kenny, Peter, Stephanie, Kerri, Frieda, and Ernie, as well as Joanne Althoff, Linda Broessel, Phyllis Cadle, Wendy Caplin, Lucy Cefalu, Kay and Bill Franey, Ted and Harriet Gottfried, Betsy and Al James, Austin Long-Scott, Carole Mayedo, Rosemarie and Marvin Mazor, Mike Sexton, and Deborah Udin.

Thanks also to Kathy Ebel and Lisa Stump for their assistance on this revision, and to my remarkable editor, E. Russell Primm.

Janet Bode's Books Speak To Teens

"When I work on a book, I try to visualize my audience," says New York City writer Janet Bode. "I see a teenager, standing in a library, struggling with a problem—and in a hurry. How can I give this reader what she or he needs? Everything in my books—content, approach, layout—follows from this image. I want my books to grab their attention."

And they do, because of their topics, nonjudgmental stance, and inventive form. By directly involving adolescents in her works-in-progress, she explores the stories behind the headlines, as well as those overlooked by the more traditional reporters.

Bode's titles, including *Beating the Odds, Kids Still Having Kids,* and *Death Is Hard to Live With,* have received numerous best-book awards from such groups as the American Library Association, the International Reading Association, and the National Council for Social Studies. *Different Worlds: Interracial and Cross-Cultural Dating* inspired a CBS-TV Schoolbreak Special, was a finalist for the NAACP Image Award, and a nominee for four daytime Emmies. "The Oprah Winfrey Show," "Larry King Live," and "20/20" are just a few of the programs on which she's appeared to discuss today's issues.

In her books, readers listen to young voices and old reminding them that while life comes with problems, there are also solutions. Ultimately in a down-to-earth manner, Janet Bode writes books of hope and inspiration.

Ida Marx Blue Spruce is a cartoonist and illustrator whose work has appeared in a wide variety of publications, among them *The New Yorker, The New Asian Times, Fantagraphics*, and the Aladdin (1997) book *Mind Riot: Coming of Age in Comix.*

Index